ROBERT SOWELL   CORNERBACK   MIAMI DOLPHINS

SO-WELL

HORACE JORDAN SR.

authorHOUSE®

AuthorHouse™
1663 Liberty Drive
Bloomington, IN 47403
www.authorhouse.com
Phone: 833-262-8899

Published by AuthorHouse 09/29/2020

ISBN: 978-1-7283-7167-2 (sc)
ISBN: 978-1-7283-7166-5 (e)

Library of Congress Control Number: 2020916353

Print information available on the last page.

This book is printed on acid-free paper.

This book is dedicated to two of the most important people in my life. To my parents, Allen and Evelyn Jordan, who gave me life and brought me up in the right way, to the best of their knowledge. I thank God for blessing you to be my parents. You were awesome role models.

Love you, Mom and Dad.

APPRECIATIONS

God comes first—without it being his will, nothing would materialize into blessings.

I would like to extend a special appreciation to the unselfish people who gave their valuable support in helping me make this book possible: Miami Dolphins football team, Miami Dolphins Publicity Department, Miami Dolphins Organization, Dave Cross, Nell and Lisa Davis, Corren Farmer, Lori Menafee Gunn, Julius and Zora Lee Hammond, James Howie, Michael Holland, Allen Jordan, Pamela Jordan, Robert Jordan, Linda Jones, Marion Jones, Robert Lawrence, Ses Levit, Ray and Bessie Martin, Larry Murrell, Chip Namias, Carol Neutzling, Mr. & Mrs. Houston Ross, Robert Sowell Jr., Thessalonia Steward, many sports writers, and all who helped me believe this book could be possible.

To my wife, Pamela Jordan; our children, Temèla Jordan, Teirra Jordan, Horace Jordan Jr.; and our grandchildren, Tyler Jordan, Tylan Jordan, Jurnee Jordan-Miller, and Athena Jordan—may your lives be filled with God's blessings.

I give special acknowledgement to Robert Bell, Deenne Hightower, Robert Sowell III, Gail Sowell, Aeriale Sowell, and Solei Sowell.

I give special thanks to Emily Smith—without your continued strengthening words of wisdom, this project may still be a plan.

Thanks again, and may we enjoy each other in a place God has prepared for us.

This book is in memory of someone very special; we only wish you were here to share the joy brought by being able to publish this book. We know you are somewhere smiling because of the accomplishment this book brings. Robert Sowell Sr., may we share joyful times in another place.

CONTENTS

CHAPTER 1

THE NIGHT SOWELL MADE THE NFL

On the breezy night of August 19, 1983, in RFK Stadium, the home of the Washington Redskins, an unknown, unheard-of free agent rookie made the NFL his home. As the Miami Dolphins arrived in Washington, only God knew that this would be the night Robert Donnell Sowell Jr. would be made one of the few selected professional football players in the NFL. For Sowell it was a dream among dreams. He knew within his heart that all he had prayed, dreamed, and lived for was on the line that night. It was a time to show the world on national television that Robert Sowell was capable of being a Miami Dolphin. The intimidation and butterflies could not interfere with the concentration he had built up since his childhood. This was his chance to live his dream—it was do or die. God had blessed Sowell with a stable mind, sound body, and great desire; it was the night to put it all together and share it with football fans.

The flight from Miami to Washington was three hours long. The team would leave Thursday morning, a day before game time. This would give the Dolphins plenty of time to get adjusted to the stadium. While the team packed their personal gear and prepared for their flight, Sowell began concentrating on the most suicidal plays in pro-football kickoff and punts on special teams.

Having to play the fifth back on the nickel defense was a worrisome job, but Sowell's mind was centered only on his first assignment: race down field at full speed when the ball was kicked off and make the tackle. It sounded easy, but in reality, it was not only hard but also dangerous. It

1

took a mind of rock, head of stone, and indestructible body to burst the wall set by the opposing teams. Sowell knew he had to go over, under, around, between, and through the wall and tackle the pigskin football. In the previous two games Sowell had been successful in tackling the ball. If in this game he had the same success, the Dolphins would have to consider him as one of the forty-five men to make the 1983 roster.

As the sixty-five players boarded this flight, which for some would be their last trip as Dolphin hopefuls, Sowell was consumed with thoughts of being with the team the rest of the season. After this game the roster would be cut down to fifty-seven men. Sowell took his seat and prepared himself for a long phase of concentration. As he looked around, the veterans seemed to show no emotions. Rookies and other players with hopes of having a job with the Dolphins were all sitting very silent. Many had already tried to start a deep sleep. Sowell's mind began to move at such a fast pace, from the game to home to practice and back to the game, that he did not know if he would be able to sleep.

Trying to listen to all the conversations around him and pretending to be calm, Sowell finally fell into a light sleep that lasted for a short while. He continued to sit with his eyes closed, pretending to be fast asleep. He felt this would make the trip much shorter. As the plane landed in the Washington airport, Sowell felt a long moment of relief. Realizing it had been a safe trip, he knew he now had to get ready and do his job. The team ate, got some rest, and went through the pregame workout. Sowell could not sleep that night. He had a shaky stomach and mild headache, all from thoughts of either making the Miami Dolphins football team or going back home to search for a job.

As the game starting time grew closer, the Dolphins made their way from the hotel to the stadium. Upon their arrival, Sowell could smell the hot dogs boiling, popcorn popping in the fresh butter, and best of all—victory. Sowell knew this was the place he wanted to be.

While putting on his uniform before going out for pregame warm-up, Sowell imagined going down the field at full speed with the force of a bulldozer and tackling the Redskins holding the pigskin football. Sowell stretched more than usual that night because he knew his plans were to run all over the field, if that was what it took to make the tackle. The goal would be to match or surpass his previous three tackles per game. But not even he knew that the game would end up showing a player resembling a wild animal on the loose, leading on special team tackles.

As the 55,045 fans began to fill the stadium, Sowell could hear them screaming and shouting. Bob Mathis and Junior Wade, the special team coaches, called to their unit for last-minute assignments. Every assignment given was part of the 167-pound player's mission. While Mathis and Wade talked, Sowell repeated in his mind, "Boom, boom, blow them over. Boom, boom, tackle the ball."

Don Shula called to the team for their last-minute pep talk. For some it would be their last talk. All eyes were on Coach Shula, but many had let their minds wander to the field. After the pep talk, there was a minute of silence for prayer. This game was either the start of the highway or the end of the road for players. For Sowell it was showtime.

The Dolphins received the ball first. This gave Sowell more time to get fired up. The game progressed, and the Dolphins scored. Now it was time to start the mission. Sowell lined up and looked down the field at the Redskin kick returner in the end zone; most likely this player would receive the ball. Sowell looked up the field; men seemed to stand ten feet tall and weigh five hundred pounds in their uniforms. He knew for sure they would be forming the wall he must destroy.

Uwe von Schamann kicked the ball, and the field began to shake. Eleven men going down the field raced at high speed toward eleven men coming up the field, all carrying masses of muscle that had taken years to build. Sowell resembled a steel ball that demolished anything in its way. Sowell's reckless play, with no concern for his body, produced another tackle. The number nineteen, a traditional quarterback number, demonstrated all kinds of skills to attack a wall or run around a wall to make the tackle. Seek, find, and destroy was what had happened to the Redskins team during Sowell's one-man kamikaze attack.

Sowell ended the first half with such a vicious tackle on a Redskin kick returner that the Miami Dolphins trainers had to assist Sowell off the field. He was cramping, and his arm had gone numb from the force used.

Sowell sat in the locker room at half time, filled with pain in parts of his body and numbness in others. To the fans and coaches, it had been a commendable performance. However, Sowell knew that games were played with two halves, not one. He could not let the pain keep him one half away from being a Dolphin. The thought of "no pain, no gain" rang in his mind.

The Dolphins' kickoff started the second half. This was Sowell's time to shine. His body felt separate from his brain, but he knew he was still in control. Despite the pain and numbness, Sowell opened the second half with yet another bruising tackle. Mathis went over to Sowell late in the game and asked if he wanted off special teams for a while. A quick "no" was Sowell's reply, for he knew if he said yes, they might sit him down and forget about him. This was another way to show the staff that he had guts and would do what it took to make the team, even if it meant playing with pain.

While in on the nickel defense, Sowell jammed a player as a screen developed and got back in time to make another terrifying tackle on a Redskin receiver. The game ended, with Sowell leading the team with six tackles. Sowell felt he had surely impressed the Dolphin staff. It demonstrated the consistency of a youngster who had his heart set on the NFL.

Back in the locker room, Sowell, filled with pain and soreness in every part of his body, had a feeling of satisfaction. But he also knew that if his all-out effort tonight did not get him a place on the team, he would have to go home and look for a job.

When interviewed about Sowell's one-man kamikaze attack, Coach Don Shula said, "That was a hell of an effort. Sowell was dehydrated and cramping, but he still threw himself at the ball carrier. It was the best effort I've ever seen on special teams." Sowell had never had a game like that before. All that had been inside him had been released. Days of pain followed, but if it was enough to make the team, it was worth every second of pain.

And make the team he did! The staff began to plan the changes that would be needed to keep Sowell on the team. He was changed to number forty-five. The press was tutored on the pronunciation of his last name. He was now considered a bonafide defensive back. The once unknown long shot had demonstrated his determination to make his dream come true. In spite of the pain, numbness, and dehydration, a dream had become reality. Friday night, August 19, 1983, proved to be the night Robert Donnell Sowell Jr. joined the select few members of the National Football League as a Miami Dolphin.

CHAPTER 2

SOWELL PRONOUNCED "SO WELL"

Robert Donnell Sowell Jr. (pronounced "so well" by his family) was born on June 23, 1961, under the sign of Cancer and was named after his father, Robert Donnell Sowell Sr. He was the second of four children born to Robert Sr. and Brenda Sowell. He had an older sister, Teres, younger brother, Stephen, and younger sister, Trina.

Many people would ask, "How is your last name pronounced? Is it Soul?"

Sowell would remark, "No. It is as if you would say, 'How are you doing?' I would say, 'So well.'" Some would say it as he said, and others would still pronounce it their way. It didn't make much difference to the determined youngster because he knew that someday he would be doing so well.

The Sowell family moved from the complex of Sullivan Garden, located on the South west side of town, to the Northeast side of Columbus. To the youth born in University Hospital, it was a sign of improvement. His dad worked hard at his job for the city and was very proud of their progress.

When Sowell nickname (Boo) became school age, he experienced many problems. Fighting occurred on just about a daily basis. He was not looking for trouble, but he did not try to avoid it either. To him it was a challenge to try to beat kids older and larger than he was. Many days Sowell would leave for school in clean, neat clothes and then return in the evening with his clothes torn and ripped, all from battles he had participated in with other kids.

When his grades began to fall below average, Sowell's teachers became concerned with his behavior. Sowell would sit during class participation time and stare out the window. When asked a question, there was no reply. Knowing that he was capable of being an above average student if he paid attention and quit "going for bad," teachers set up parent-teacher conferences. This seemed to get Sowell back into his schoolwork for only a short while.

As Sowell's skills in sports developed, his school studies fell behind even more. By fifth grade the only things on his mind were sports and competition. In the summer of 1973, he scrounged around until he found some weights. This would be the year he would attempt to play recreational football. During that summer he stayed off the streets more. Running and lifting weights proved to take up most of the growing youngster's time. For him a dream of professional sports was in the making.

In the spring the school held sixth graders' field day. This matched the sixth grade classes with each other, and most importantly for Sowell, it matched student against student. This was his chance to show the school how athletic he was. Being a winner at an event would place that student as the best in the school. Each class was allowed time, usually the last period of the day, to practice for the event. After school Sowell went home and practiced even more. He figured he would win at least one running event because of his running experience as a youth at The Ohio State University Stadium and Arlington Park Recreation Center.

The competition began on a hot May day. Sowell competed in the 600-yard run, the 600-yard relay, and the high jump. For him it was a disappointing day in the running events. Sowell did not win either running event, and his class did not win the overall competition. But when the dust all cleared and the classes retired to the lunchroom for refreshments, Sowell had finished as the winner and best high jumper in the school, even after falling and spraining his wrist on his last jump. This accomplished some of what Sowell had wanted to prove to the school: he could be the best at something he did. This also encouraged him to continue to compete in sports; he could someday excel at something.

The transition from elementary school to junior high was an even greater challenge. Just as Sowell improved, others did too. He was also trying to improve his grades. Talking with school counselors, Sowell was advised that if he did not improve his grades, no matter how good he was in sports, he would never make it. He had heard this many times from many different people. However, these words would still not turn him away from his dream of being a professional athlete. He continued to run, lift, and train hard, but he studied little.

By his sophomore year, Sowell realized that school had to be completed. If an athlete's grades were not on the whole passing, he or she would not be able to participate in sports. Sowell knew then that he would not be able to play football if he did not concentrate on his studies. This may have very well been one of the best things to happen to Sowell as a student. His grades improved to an average student level, and the problems of "hanging out" because of free time took a turn for the better. His love for sports made him do anything to compete, even spend time with schoolwork.

After Sowell quit the football team his sophomore year, he found the fall to be a long troublesome one for him. He was at the age of being able to drive, but not having a job, he was unable to afford a car, unlike many other teenagers. He had to rely on the use of the family car. When wanting to date girls, he had to do odd jobs to get enough money for the date and gas money for the tank and then hope his dad didn't have any plans. Not being able to use the car much, Sowell had to do more walking and jogging to see his girlfriend.

After sitting idle for a season and watching professional football, Sowell's dream of being there started to haunt him again. He decided to make all the bad work for him. When unable to get the car to go somewhere, he would jog. The fear of being jailed or getting hurt in a fight that could hamper his chances of playing football made him turn from releasing frustration in fights to lifting weights in his front yard.

Sowell decided college would be his next route after high school. That would mean no more hanging out; he needed to do schoolwork and keep in shape with all of his extra time. His grades for the next two years of school must maintained a passing mark. He knew he didn't want to attend a junior college; he wanted to get into a big college and play big-time football. During the evening hours, when not studying, he would train. It all paid off for him when he was accepted to Howard University. It was the opportunity to play college football and get an education.

After the first semester of his freshman year of college, Sowell was forced to make one of the biggest decisions of his young life. He felt that he was needed at home. His father had become ill and was unable to help his son with the extra needs he had as a college student without a job. In the winter of 1979 Sowell returned home to look for a job and make a living the best he could. Not wanting to give up on his dream, he planned to return to school and play football when finances got better; however, finding a job that winter proved to be a lost cause. In the spring he decided to attend a small school to learn a trade. He learned to clean, wax, buff, and do small repairs on automobiles. This training produced a job that helped him get his first car, a maroon, two-door Lincoln Town Car. Life seemed to be falling into good prospective for Sowell. But this would only last for a short while, for dark days were sure to come again.

Just when things seemed to be going good for the young adult, a dark cloud covered his life. When it rose, Sowell had no car, job, or money to go back to school. This would prove to be the start of his special mission. He became even more determined to accomplish his dream of making it to the pro ranks of football. Skipping over the years of eligibility he had left in college, because the money he had anticipated wasn't there, Sowell set his sights on professional football. He knew it would take pure strength, the willingness to absorb pain, and an untouchable burning desire to succeed. Training now would be first on his list. It would be his job that paid off at a later date.

Sowell felt that he had what it took, and with hard work, he could develop into a professional defensive back in the NFL. He knew that he was too gifted and talented to settle for a job as a laborer in a plant or a car cleaner on a car lot. He knew, just like many other young football players, that if he did not reach for the stars, he would never fulfill his destiny. That destiny would bring big money, a popular name, many admiring fans admiring, kids looking up to him, and most of all, the comfort of a glamorous lifestyle—things nobody else in his neighborhood had experienced. All this and more would come in the package of a professional athlete.

Sowell knew he would gain the respect of others. Many would be proud of him. He would be that one in a million to make it. And when asked, "How are you doing?" he could reply, "I'm doing so well!"

CHAPTER 3

REJECTED PEEWEE

When a youth gets cut from a team at the first attempt, it typically causes that person to look at other activities. A youngster determined to make it even after rejection, Sowell did not let his stroke of bad luck change his plans. In early July of 1973 a 12 year old, six grader Robert Sowell walked over to St. Gabriel School to begin his mission to conquer the game of football. But it wasn't anything like he planned. After only a few days of running and tackling a hanging stuffed dummy, the coaches of the Cardinals informed Sowell that his services with the team would not be needed. Feeling rejected as he took the long way home, Sowell tried to hold back the tears that showed the hurt on his face. He knew down inside that they had made a mistake. He knew that if someone had taken the time to teach him, he could develop what it took to play football.

After a week of watching other players and practicing at home in his backyard, Sowell decided to make another bid to play football that season. With the Audubon Chargers practicing just fifteen minutes from his home, he decided it would be the next close team from the three-minute walk of the Cardinals. The Chargers were not a strong team. Many called them a scrub team that was not for real, but that didn't matter to Sowell.

From the opening of the season, the Chargers knew it would be a long and painful one for them. They opened with a loss and then a tie to a team that was missing eight starters at game time. The third game proved to be the turning point for the Chargers, as they downed the North Glen Chiefs in a hard-fought shutout. This victory inspired the team and Sowell, for they had overcome the thought of participating in a winless season.

For Sowell, it inspired him to continue on with the game he so desired to succeed at.

The team continued to improve as the season progressed, as did Sowell. Many of the players looked forward to the match with the St. Gabriel Cardinals. This game brought strong anticipation for the Chargers, who had improved their record to 2–3–1. In the seventh week of the nine-week schedule, the Chargers proved to be a competitive team that was for real. They were prepared to face the undefeated Cardinals. A win over the Cardinals could make their season. The game, played at Audubon Field number two, proved to be a rivalry, both teams playing for pride. Sowell was moved from offensive lineman to quarterback because of the injury of the regular starting quarterback. The tall, thin player would finally get to show his talent.

From the start Sowell knew that the transition he had made to team leader was a costly one. Not being able to move his team up the field frustrated him. When going back to pass, he was sacked several times. Always wanting to run the ball, Sowell began to want to dish the punishment out. His team fell way short as they were shut out, 21–0, by a strong powerhouse team. The pain he felt again from the Cardinal organization burned deep inside his bones. While walking off the field, with pain and soreness suffered from being tackled several times, Sowell promised himself that he would never feel rejected again. From then on, he would dish out the punishment.

The season ended with the Chargers finishing above two other teams, with a 3–5–1 record. Sowell, a youth with the desire to play football, did not let the poor season change his dreams. Instead he learned to better prepare himself for the next season of football.

Gaining weight to his slim frame and aging another year forced Sowell to move up to an older and heavier weight class of players. The weight increase from 85 pounds and under to 105 pounds and under meant even tougher competition. Sowell joined the Northern Steelers, who were just minutes away from his old team. The Steelers were basically a new team in the league ruled by the Linden Eagles and East Side YMCA Tigers (Y). The Steelers arranged a scrimmage game with the Y, which proved to be too soon for the Steelers. The Y jumped all over the Steelers, beating them, 33–0. This did not discourage the team or Sowell, for he had been down that road many times before in the previous season with the Chargers. Sowell hoped that the rest of the season would be nothing like the beating they took in that scrimmage.

To everyone's surprise, by the season end Sowell and the Steelers had complied a 7–0 record, scoring 139 points and allowing only 15, second to the undefeated Y with 254 points scored. The Steelers' record put them in the playoff game against the Sertoma Jets with a 3–4–0 record. The Y faced the West Gate Golden Eagles with a 5–1–1 record, their only loss coming early in the season to the Y, the only team to score on them. The Steelers and the Y both won and proved to be worthy of a championship berth.

On November 2, 1974, the two undefeated teams battled at Mohawk Stadium. The scrimmage from early in the season seemed far behind. For Sowell, playing in his first championship game would be a complete turnaround from just a short year ago. During that week of practice, both teams worked long and hard, knowing the outcome could go either way. The Y took an early lead, 6–0, and scored again before the half. Down twelve points at halftime meant the Steelers would have to play harder the second half. Sowell was just pleased to be on a team and playing in a championship game. In the fourth quarter the Y extended the lead to nineteen points to secure the victory. With only minutes remaining to be played, the Steelers finally lit the scoreboard with a touchdown. But it was too little too late, as they fell short 19–6 to the stronger Y team. Sowell thought of how he had made a team and played in a championship, which led him to think that maybe next time he would be with the winners.

When the 1975 Y team opened their practice, Sowell was in attendance. He practiced with the Y for about a week. The team heads had a meeting, since so many players changed teams. Some teams had too many players, while others didn't have enough. The league officials agreed that no player who had played the previous year could participate with another team unless a coach signed a release form. Sowell had hoped to be released, but after his coach watched in a practice session, he was convinced he would help put the Steelers in the championship again. Sowell decided that playing where he had played before might be the best for him. Maybe it would be good for him to play for the team that helped develop him.

The season opened with a rematch of the defending champion East Side YMCA Tigers and the Northern Steelers. It was a new year and a new game held at Krumm Park. It was a hot day, but Sowell would be playing in the defensive lineup, the place he had so desired to be. His gained weight and height would help him bring the big running backs down. With this being 115 pounds and under, most backs were as heavy as their linemen.

The game was a game of defense, as neither team scored in the first half of play. The second half was pretty much the same, until late in the fourth quarter the Steelers maintained a drive and scored. The extra point was unsuccessful, but the touchdown proved to be the game winner. The Steelers had pulled off the upset, 6–0. It was the first time in three years the Y had lost and only the second in five years that they had been shut out. Most of the Steelers felt a feeling of power. For Sowell it was the beginning of a new and fulfilling sensation for the sport of football.

Sowell and his teammates continued the roll and finished the season undefeated for the second year in a row. Winning the playoff insured a replay of last season's championship game, only this time the Steelers were favored. The Steelers captured an early 12–0 lead for only minutes, as the Y came rolling back with a touchdown before the half ended. The game continued as both teams' defenses destroyed the other's offense. Late in the fourth quarter it seemed as if the Y would score and pull the victory off. But the Steelers contained, and the game ended, 12–7, with the Steelers victorious. For Sowell it was the reason for being there, a short turnaround of just two years ago. He was now on the right road and enjoying the high spirits of a champ. Most of all, he was keeping his promise to himself of not being rejected again.

CHAPTER 4

QUIT, BUT DON'T GIVE UP

Robert Sowell thought that quitting football as a sophomore in high school was one of the biggest regrets he would have to live with, after realizing that getting a starting job as a varsity defensive back for the Mifflin Punchers proved to be a harder task than he had anticipated. From day one of spring practice, Sowell felt not only the July heat from the sun but also the heat of all the upper-class seniors. They were determined not to let any sophomores (underclassmen) have a starting role on the team. This brought fear to Sowell and other underclassmen because they were so much smaller than their teammates. During station drills, where the coaches had each player one on one or two on one, the seniors took advantage of the size and experience they had over the underclassmen. But when it came time to scrimmage and it was eleven on eleven, the underclassmen exceled. From defensive back position, Sowell made some head-shaking tackles that made the coaches take note of him as a starter. The upperclassmen, sensing this, took all means not to let him continue to play at that pace. The use of intimidation became a must with the upperclassmen. They would use foul language, talk about family members, and even take cheap shots after the whistle had blown. These tactics proved to encourage Sowell's early departure.

As the heat rose from the forties during morning practices to the scorching eighties by evening drills, Sowell drew weary of his teammates' behavior. Finally, Sowell felt he could take no more of the unteamly behavior. He turned his equipment in and looked forward to the next season of football. This decision was painful for the youth, who had felt himself excelling enough to fill a starting role. To let go of his dream and watch another player play the position that he was capable of playing made the hardship even more unbearable. The disappointment did not push him away as others thought. He thought back to when he was a peewee and was rejected. At least this time he had some say in the decision. For Sowell it was just another phase he had to deal with. He could not allow the love of the sport to be placed too far away in his mind. Therefore, he began to concentrate on the next season.

The high school team had a poor season, finishing with a 2–7–0 record, one of the worst in the league. For some it was the end of a high school career of Friday Nightmares. For Sowell and others, who planned to return to the Punchers squad next year, it was already time to begin conditioning.

The winter of 1976 and spring of 1977 proved Sowell was not to be picked on again. During the winter Sowell worked on his speed and strength. Day by day, drill by drill, thinking of cheering crowds, bands playing, and the pads smacking together on Friday nights made Sowell work himself to the limit.

After his walking away as a sophomore, none expected to see Sowell out for football again. But during the early morning hours Sowell was in his front yard lifting weights. For him it was all done for a purpose. Others felt it was a waste of his time. Defensive Coach Don Eppert knew Sowell had talent. He explained that Sowell was heck of a player if he would just stick it out and not let others turn him away. He knew Sowell had what it took and just needed to develop his skills more. Sowell couldn't let the others bring him down.

Sowell began carrying a football around with him from tenth grade on, as reminder of his goal. He carried it wherever he went. He took it along to discos, restaurants, even to work when he could find an odd job to do. When he went to bed, he hugged it like it was a pillow. Some people thought he was strange. At times his parents thought he was losing his mind. Neighbors shook their heads when they saw him jogging around early in the morning and late at night with his football.

When spring of 1977 came around and the Punchers began their sessions twice a day, a youngster once turned away stood proud among his teammates. Sowell knew this was a new him. After gaining weight and getting faster over the winter from running track, he wasn't going to let anyone turn him away again from his dream. Practice sessions were pretty much the same this season, except Sowell and other classmates were not considered underclassmen now. They had experienced so much torment the previous year that they seemed to have more control than the seniors. During drills and stations, Sowell excelled as he had a year earlier. He worked hard, and the coaches were pleased with his progress. He was placed at the defensive back position that he had dreamed of playing, like his idol Oakland Raider Jack Tatum. He began playing physical, taking every opportunity to make contact with anyone in his path to the ball.

Starting both as a wingback on offense and safety on defense, Sowell had little time to rest. As a junior, it gave him the opportunity to make up the time that he had missed out on in his sophomore year. Every play could be a deciding factor. He met the challenge with intentions to conquer.

In the season opener on September 10, 1977, against Utica at Utica, Sowell played the whole game, only resting in the huddle between plays and at halftime. Without the strength conditioning drills during the year layoff, he might have passed out on the field. Hoping to help the team to victory, he was part of numerous tackles, but when time ran out and the game ended, the scoreboard read the same as it had at the beginning of the game: 0–0. The two teams had played to a scoreless tie.

The next two weeks showed even less of a chance for the Punchers to have a successful season, as they were shut out both weeks. When the Punchers returned home for parents' night on September 30, the fans were there in numbers to see why their team had not won a game or scored any points. Sowell, knowing his parents and other family members were in attendance, felt he must have a good night. In the first series of plays he accomplished a bit of what he wanted to show by catching a pass and racing sixty yards to the end zone, for a score that electrified the fans. For the first time that season, the Punchers were on the scoreboard and out in front of the opposing team. The fans were out of control anticipating a victory. But as the game progressed, the Punchers found themselves falling behind and losing 18–8. Memories of the peewee Chargers and their poor season became a strong thought in Sowell's mind. However, he knew if he stuck it out, things would soon change.

On October 7, at home against the East High Tigers, the Punchers put their winless record behind them and played on school pride. The locker room was filled with a mist that was unusual for the Punchers. They knew they wanted nothing more than to beat the Tigers in front of the home crowd. The game proved to be physical from the very beginning, with both teams dishing out terrifying hits. Sowell began to feel the urge to get loose and concentrate on his defensive play. Now playing defense only, Sowell felt that he could excel much more. He wanted this game to be his best, and at halftime it was evident that it would be. He was leading the team in tackles from his deep back position. He had two batted away passes and an interception. He proved that he had the desire and the ability to hit and make things happen. All night long he followed the ball and made tackles all over the field to help secure the Punchers' first victory of the season, 12–7, over the Tigers at home.

After losing the next two games, one a shutout, the team decided the remaining two games must be played on pride. With their record now 1–4–1, the Punchers took to the field against the Mohawk Raiders, a team also having a poor season. Both teams were looking for a victory in the Punchers' last home game of the season. Sowell's wanted to keep his head up and play to the best of his ability, even if neither team could finish with a decent record. He still would play it as if it were a championship game.

The Punchers took an early lead with a quick touchdown and continued to build on it as the game progressed. By halftime the Punchers were up, 13–0, and on their way to their second victory of the season. The team proved that with pride players still can show ability, if they try. Sowell, with excellent defensive play, helped the Punchers shut out their opponents, 20–0. His consistent play showed that a player with heart can excel. Leading in tackles, causing three fumbles, and snagging an interception were all proof of that.

The final game of the season saw the Punchers fall short to the Linden McKinley Panthers, 25–12, the team that went on to win the city league championship. To Sowell and the Punchers, it was a disappointment, finishing with two wins, six losses, and a tie. Again, it was one of the worst records in the league.

Sowell finished the season with such a convincing record of stats that he was named to the all-city team as a junior. This was a great achievement for a player who had quit a year earlier and was now on a team that had two straight poor seasons.

Sowell's senior year should have been his best, as he was looking forward to playing major college football the following year. Sowell showed up to practice in top condition. He felt the pressure of not only being a senior but also being a returning starter, who lettered and had been named to the all-city team. He concentrated on having a super season on defense, so colleges would take note of him. Not only did he want to excel on the field, but he also realized that he must excel in the classroom if he was to receive a scholarship from a major university. This meant studying along with practices and getting help if needed in schoolwork. He would not be considered just an athlete but a student as well.

Setting the pace in team practices and sprints, Sowell showed he wanted to be a team leader. Before the season opener, Sowell was chosen as one of the team's captains. The Punchers opened their season against the Polar Bears of North High School at North. The Punchers had not won their opening game since they had played in the city league championship three years earlier. For the seniors it was a must win to change the losing efforts they had been experiencing. The first half of play seemed to hold the same old pattern, ending with neither team scoring. In the locker room Sowell and other captains took charge and talked to the underclassmen. They did not want to go out as losers as their upperclassmen had done. The team decided that they would pull it together and go out and win the game. In the third quarter the Punchers lit the scoreboard up with a touchdown following the first of Sowell's three interceptions, which set a new school record for most interceptions in one game. Sowell continued to plague the Polar Bear's offense with punishing tackles and ended the third quarter with his second interception that froze a Polar Bear scoring drive.

The fourth quarter proved to be the quencher for the Punchers' lead, 6–0. Both teams battled, knowing it could be anyone's game. The Polar Bears were on a drive in the Punchers' territory and threatening to score with less than a minute to play in the game. Sowell positioned himself, knowing the Bears had to pass. If he had any chance to get the ball, he would. The Polar Bear quarterback faded back and released the pass, trying to score and make the extra point to win the game. Every fan in the stands on both sides was on their feet. When the ball was caught, guess who was on the receiving end? Sowell was, with his third and record-breaking interception that he ran back to the Polar Bears' thirty-three-yard line to preserve the Punchers' victory.

Smelling the victory now, the Punchers had time for one more play, and they wanted another score to make the win look more convincing. On the last play of the game, the Punchers got just that, with a thirty-three-yard touchdown, a thriller for Sowell and teammates as they shut out the Polar Bears 12–0.

Feeling the thrill of victory, Sowell knew he was finally getting to be where he wanted to be. His schoolwork had showed improvement, and he was showing leadership.

The next week the Punchers hosted the East High Tigers at home. Sowell was hyped up for the game after being named defensive player of the week the previous Friday night. Going both ways again for Sowell would show his fitness. Now with the college scouts concentrating on him, he needed to show that he could play the whole game on the offense and defense, if needed. The half ended in a scoreless tie. Both teams were playing with reckless abandon but with no touchdowns. In the final half of play the Tigers opened the scoring with a touchdown and ended it with a field goal, handing the Punchers their first loss in front of the home crowd, 10–0.

For the seniors, it was hard to handle the loss, knowing they had taken the Tigers too lightly. It seemed to sidetrack some of the players. Some seniors decided they were going to cut practice. Coach Orth warned them that if they did, they would not play in Friday night's game against the Centennial Stars. Being a team captain and having received a few letters from major colleges, Sowell felt that he was a star now, and if he missed practice, he would still be allowed to play. When practice was held, Sowell and two other senior starters were not in attendance. When seen in school the next day, they were notified that they would not dress or play in the game. For the now superstar, Sowell, this was a shocker. He could not believe the team would play without him. But when Friday night came, not only did the Punchers play without Sowell, they also beat the Stars at Centennial by a runaway score of 25–6, boosting their record to two wins with only one loss.

When practice began after school the next week, Sowell and all others were in attendance. He wasn't going to cut practice again to just hang out with friends. He knew he had made a big mistake that could cost him extra stats to better his bid for the college ranks. He learned that no matter how good a player is, one has to practice if he intends to play. He now wanted to get back on the field after watching his team coast to an easy victory. It hurt him almost as much as sitting out a whole year. That experience helped the star to come back down to earth. Winning his starting job back on offense and defense in just two practice sessions by exhausting himself in drills and making crushing tackles, he didn't want to be used as an example again.

September 29 at home was parents' night for the Punchers. On the first play Sowell caught a pass from his wide receiver spot and raced forty yards into the end zone for a Puncher score. Following that touchdown with an interception on defense, it seemed as if the Punchers were on their way to another blowout. In the final half it was all the Braves as the Punchers fell behind and lost, 19–6, despite playing a hard game.

The team, with two wins and two losses, were still determined to have a good season. Finally receiving a long-awaited letter from The Ohio State Buckeyes, Sowell started to concentrate more on his defensive play and his schoolwork. Studying after practice and getting help from the teachers between classes and during free periods, he saw his grades begin to show major college level ability.

The next three weeks were a nightmare for the Punchers, as they lost their homecoming game and two others on the road by shutouts. Still Sowell's stats hung up top with other outstanding players in central Ohio. Now in the top five in the state, with six interceptions, he was a sought-after athlete.

On October 26 the Punchers traveled to Linden McKinley to take on the previous year's city league champion Panthers. Now at wing back on offense, Sowell was able to carry the ball more, showing he was a versatile player. The game proved to be a come from behind thriller and the highlight of the season for the Punchers—the most memorable in Sowell's high school career. The Punchers, with two wins and five losses and trailing at halftime, 14–0, decided it was time to show what they had worked so hard to be. They came out smoking and scored two quick touchdowns to bring them within two points. Both teams played tough ball down to the final seconds. The Punchers were trailing, 12–14, with only seconds left and the ball on the two-yard line, second and goal. Sowell tried entering the end zone twice but was stopped short both times. With fourth down and goal, the ball resting on the one-yard line and only nine seconds to play, the Punchers knew it was roothog or die. Holding hands in the huddle as a sign of unity,

Sowell was given the last crack at a score and victory for the Punchers. He felt the team had faith in him because they elected not to try an easy field goal that would have won the game. With the outcome of the game resting on his shoulders, Sowell assured the offensive line that he would carry the ball across if they blocked their man for just one second. It seemed to be the longest yard that a team had to travel. The team broke the huddle with determination to be winners. When the ball was snapped, the line did their job of keeping the Panthers out of the backfield. Sowell took the handoff and drove as high and straight over the top as he could, determined not to be stopped until he reached the end zone. When he finally came down from his flight to victory, the Punchers were awarded a touchdown and had come from behind to defeat the Panthers. Walking off the field with two touchdowns, one interception, and numerous tackles, Sowell was satisfied with his performance and happy to have family bragging rights over his cousin that played for the Panthers.

November 3, 1978, at home against the Bearcats of Brookhaven, the seniors and Sowell had their final performance as Punchers at Mifflin High School. Some would go on to play at major colleges, some would play at small colleges, and for some it would be the end of the road for football. The Bearcats took an early lead, 7–0, but the Punchers came right back with a score to even the game up. Minutes before halftime, the Bearcats scored again to take the lead at halftime, 14–7. In the locker room at halftime the level of intensity was high. There was no tomorrow or next year for many. In Sowell's case he didn't want to go out the same way he had come in: a quitter. He wiped his face and geared up for a hard second half.

The Punchers kicked off to start the half. On the first play, Sowell came up to make a smashing tackle and followed up the next play with a batted away pass. This got the team fired up. The Punchers got the ball back and tied the score 14–14. Both teams started to wear down from the hard contact that was being dished out and absorbed on the field. In the fourth quarter the Bearcats managed a touchdown from a Puncher turnover. The Punchers still refused to give up after turning the ball back over to the Bearcats on downs deep in Bearcat territory. The defense dug in and tackled the Bearcats quarterback in the end zone for a safety and two points. The Bearcats kicked off to the Punchers, who now only trailed by five points, 21–16. The Punchers quickly drove down field but were unable to score before time ran out. It was too little too late as it ended, 21–16, in favor of the Bearcats.

For the Punchers it was another disappointing season. For Sowell he looked forward to college football. He wished his team would have done better, but he accepted his honors of all-city (for the second year), all-metro, and all-Ohio, and he started thinking of what college he would attend. He figured his achievements would get him a job as a defensive back in college. That's where he wanted to be: giving out punishment, not receiving it. But first he had to complete his senior year of school and graduate.

As the school year progressed and the offers of a full-ride scholarship were not forthcoming, Sowell's grades and outlook on life took a quick 180-degree turn for worse. Being confused with his life now and not participating in any sport or activities, Sowell's grades dropped, and he began to hang out and waste time, not knowing where he was going to play his college career. The thought of being offered a scholarship by The Ohio State football coach, Woody Hayes, and then the offer being reconsidered and withdrawn by the new coach, Earl Bruce, was more than Sowell could bear.

In the spring of 1979 Sowell realized that all professional players didn't come from a few colleges. If he proved himself, no matter where he did it, he might get a chance to fulfill his goal: to play professional football. But by then his grades were too low to be considered. Many colleges started asking him to attend a junior college first and then go join their team. Sowell, being determined from childhood, knew if there was a will, there was a way. He knew he could improve his grades and prepare himself for a major college right after high school.

Sowell went out for wrestling to keep in shape. The conditioning for wrestling was more strenuous on the body than other sports he had participated in. He knew it would improve his strength, along with his weightlifting program. Wrestling in competition for the first time was hard. Not being able to use his street fighting ability, Sowell had to wrestle by the high school rules. This turned him away from wrestling and back to track, another favorite sport. He decided to hit the weights harder and run track to get himself prepared for college. Long hours of study and a great deal of extra time from teachers helped Sowell to bring his grades up to average level, a level that would attract college scouts.

One of the six seniors on the track team, Sowell worked hard to position himself in an individual spot. He earned 142.5 season points and qualified for the state meet in the long jump and three-hundred-meter low hurdles, with a school and city record time of 37.8 seconds. Sowell entered the state meet as an expected winner in at least one event but had trouble in the long jump and didn't place. He then concentrated on breaking his own record and winning the low hurdles. All seemed to be going well until the final heat, with the top eight runners racing for the state title. Sowell got off to a good start and seemed to have the race won, but when he got to the last hurdle, he tripped and fell. When he returned to his feet, not wanting to give up, he limped to the finish line to finish sixth, with a time of 40.9 seconds. This was another disappointment for the youngster after having done such a good job during the season. To fall short in the big race brought tears to his eyes. He didn't go home a loser all the way around because the Punchers still won the state AA track championship. After his second effort performance that showed he wasn't going to stay down if he fell, the scouts really tried to recruit him.

As graduation neared, Sowell felt he had reached a well-waited, hard-fought end of a high school career as an athlete, and it was time to buckle down and play with the big guys from here on out. Though his size wasn't what he wished, it was a solid 5'10" and 160 pounds. He felt his strength and speed would make up the difference. He had learned that with determination and burning desire, it was possible to overcome some hardships and make a good impression. Sowell elected to attend Howard University upon graduation.

When accepted, Sowell was behind in classes because the school was unable to find his transcript, but he worked hard to catch up. He figured if he concentrated on his studies as a freshman, by the time he was a sophomore or junior, he could really make a break into the lineup; his grades wouldn't hinder him. When Sowell arrived at Howard and attended practice, he experienced the same problems and pressures he had as a sophomore in high school. Many players were much bigger, stronger, and even faster than he was. But he wasn't going to be turned away. He had experienced success and felt the pain of failure. He knew it was more painful to watch than get out there and play. Knowing the players weren't going to get smaller gave him that feeling of competition that he once possessed and thrived on. He battled with everyone that got in his way, until the coaches decided to give him some playing time in the games. They placed him just where he wanted to be in the defensive secondary. Being only a freshman, his time was limited, but when he was in the game, he made things happen for the Bison defense. In one game against North Carolina Central University (NCCU), Sowell had two interceptions and tackles with force that helped spark the Bison to a 31–20 lead at the half.

The Bison coaching staff had high hopes for their talented freshman and awaited his return the next season. Even after making second team all-conference as a freshman, the darkest and miserable days of Sowell's life began. After Sowell's father, Robert Sr., became very ill Robert Jr. felt he was needed at home. He decided to put his dream on hold and return home, with the hopes of coming back to school when things at home got better. He thought he could quit but not give up.

CHAPTER 5

JUST AN INTERRUPTION

For a football player who experienced the hype of high school stardom and the glory of an excelling freshman in college, the darkest and loneliest days of Sowell's interrupted life came when he decided to pack his bags and return home—not knowing this period would last three years. After only one semester of school and one season of crushing football for the Howard Bisons, Sowell joined the real world, a world of working to make a decent living unless you became lucky and won money or someone died and left you an inheritance.

The winter of 1980 was to be a long and jobless one for an athlete who had seemed to be on his way to an easy, high-paying job as a professional football player. Not able to support himself as an adult and wanting to be able to prove himself as a responsible man made each day colder than the day before. He got up every morning and started out looking for a job, hoping that one would come his way. His father was weak from his sickness, and Sowell's unemployment was a burden on the family. He felt he must find a way to at least support himself or there wasn't any reason to be at home again, since the main reason for his return home was to help out the family as his dad recovered from his illness.

Going from building to building, hoping that somebody somewhere could use his services, depressed Sowell more and more. He wanted so much to be his own man. After many unsuccessful tries to land a job and knowing he was not ready to go back to Howard University, he decided to try another approach to life. After hearing about a trade school on Cleveland Avenue, he decided to get involved in some activities that might benefit him. He signed up for a course to learn how to clean and paint cars. With training, he could become qualified for a job. Most employers were reluctant to hire applicants without training in a specific area.

Returning to class again made Sowell feel that he was on his way to success. He rose every morning and went off to school, anticipating competition, getting a job, and even owning the car he had dreamed of. Each day of classes taught something new. He wished that the cars he practiced on were his own. He knew if he ever got a car, he would do his best to keep it looking good at all times.

After completion of the course, he applied for numerous jobs until he was finally contacted to interview for a position. At the interview he had to present his certificate to prove completion of the course and then demonstrate what he had learned.

When hired for the job, everything seemed to fall right in place. Sowell was finally able to consider getting a car of his own. After he found a car that he liked, he experienced the problem of having someone cosign, since he had not been able to establish credit. It seemed almost as difficult as getting a job. However, he had faith and exhausted all means. He went to friends and neighbors, relatives, and even former teachers and coaches. After almost giving up, he had a stroke of luck and was able to obtain the 1975 two door Lincoln Continental that he had dreamed of owning. Now, instead of always cleaning a car and watching the owner drive it away, he was able to enjoy the pleasure of riding away in the driver's seat. Sowell felt he could finally say, "This is mine. I am finally on the right road of life."

Having his own wheels made life a bit easier. Sowell was able to get back and forth from place to place without the hassle of asking for a ride or walking. Going to work was also more fulfilling because now he had something to work for and show for his work. All seemed to be in good order, but little did Sowell know that having a big car, if not used wisely, could create big problems. After a hard week of work, Sowell would clean up his car and go out on the town. In and out of nightspots Sowell would go, as many as he could find. bright nightlife. Sowell had to decide what was important in his life. Working during the day and partying at night gave Sowell little time to think about what he really wanted to be. It seemed as if he was content with the way life was. The dream of being a famous professional football player seemed to no longer exist. People asked him, "Are you still going to play football? Are you still going back to college?" He would laugh and reply with the affirmative but not with the ring of determination and desire that his voice once possessed.

Sowell's lifestyle had changed, and now the name of the game was hanging with the crowd and being cool. (That's all he had to do to get his peers to accept him.) The sense of having people look up to him made Sowell feel secure with his life. He lost all means of wanting to be an idol of many.

Staying out late at night and driving around after the clubs closed soon caught up with him. Sowell began to report to work late or even take the entire day off. Soon he developed the attitude that if others could make it without working, so could he. Not being satisfied with his job after a while, he returned to the unemployment ranks.

Sowell quickly discovered that having a big car, dressing in fine clothes, and taking dates out on the town were costly. Without employment and not doing some kind of illegal operation, he just couldn't survive too much longer.

When the bills began to back up on Sowell and he was unable to find work or get help from friends and relatives, he awakened to the real world. However, by that time he was so far behind that even a regular job couldn't help him get caught up. The big dream reappeared in his mind once again. This time he knew he needed a strong helper, a keeper that would stand by him no matter how rough times got. He needed someone with an inner strength that would help him reach his highest goal, someone that would help him accept what was meant to be and help him make any necessary changes to become a better person and stronger mentally, physically, and spiritually. The only source from which he could obtain such help was God. Sowell turned to the Almighty for help and assurance.

Life did not change overnight because Sowell wanted the Lord in his life. However, destiny did make some adjustments. After putting God first in his life, change was noticeable. Down and out in life doesn't mean a person should hide in a corner or roll over and die. It is then that one learns to appreciate all the little luxuries of life. Now back to the weights and running, he knew it was time for him to continue his mission. With determination to be a success, he ran mile after mile and lifted weights twice a day. Eating as many times as possible each day to gain weight, he started planning to play the game he loved.

When hearing of various tryouts for the USFL and NFL teams,

Sowell worked even harder, believing some team would be able to use his experience. Going to Canada was a joyful occasion for the athlete, but after he got there and was turned down because they felt his legs were too weak and he was too young at nineteen years, he became depressed. He later was advised to join up with one of their affiliated semi-pro teams, the Twin City Cougars in Sacramento, California. Sowell was paid fifty dollars a week, and he was also given room and board and placed on the food stamp role. It was a long way from what he had intended, but it was a start. Making eight of nine tackles for the Cougars in one game on the special teams, he started the pattern that proved to be the key. Knocking himself out showed Sowell was hungry for the ball carriers. Strengthening his legs and playing like he was getting a million dollars a year kept him on the team and helped the Cougars to win the semi-pro national championship. Once again, he had performed with the best.

The following season the Cougars informed Sowell they would not be able to afford to renew his contract. But for him it didn't matter because his college class was graduating. Now he would finally be eligible to try out for an NFL team. In the NFL, an individual could not join the team until his class had graduated. In the USFL and Canadian football there were no such limitations.

Sowell hoped to play for the Chicago Blitz of the USFL, a team that had seemed to be interested in him, but they later reneged on a deal. Sowell and his girlfriend then decided to exhaust all means. She typed résumés, and they sent them to all twenty-eight NFL teams and twelve USFL clubs, hoping to hear good news from some of the ball clubs about a free agent getting a tryout.

After a long period of time, responses started coming in. Pittsburgh, San Francisco, and Tampa Bay said they were not giving any free agent tryouts. The Colts wrote and told him they had enough people but wished him luck in the future. Houston, Detroit, and New Orleans wrote they were interested, but they didn't follow through. Many other teams didn't bother to send a response. The Dolphins' Charlie Winner actually called. Soon after the phone call, the Dolphins scout and former Buffalo Bills speedster Elbert Dubenion came and watched Sowell workout.

After going through some drills and taking times in the forty-yard dash, Dubenion advised Sowell to continue to train and maybe he would hear from them again. Dubenion informed Winners of the ability he felt Sowell had. After going over his résumé and finding he matched up, the Dolphins felt they could use Sowell in their preseason camp. Finally, after a three-year period of only dreaming of what he could do if given a chance, Sowell would get that chance—even if only to say, "I had my shot at being a professional football player in the NFL."

What seemed to be a hard battle to achieve a goal proved to be the easiest stage of Sowell's career. The difficult part would be trying to get prepared to challenge players that outweighed him by one hundred pounds. He was to compete against college all-Americans with four years of experience in college competition.

The young man had finally come to the road in his life that so many had started on but never completed. He could put all the interruptions in life behind him and exert himself to achieve a goal that others would have given up on.

CHAPTER 6

PSYCHO CONDITIONING TO GO

S owell conditioned for eight hours a day, seven days a week; it was a job that would pay at a later date. Using a strenuous exercising program and mind psyching techniques is what qualified Sowell for a worthwhile tryout with Don Shula and the Miami Dolphins. Everyone who watched Sowell jogging in the rain, sleet, and snow, at temperatures often below freezing, felt he was living in a fantasy world. For Sowell it was bringing him mile by mile closer to a career of professional football.

Knowing that his days as a collegiate player were cut short, he knew he must reach to the sky and think of no limits to reaching his fullest potential. Sowell knew that if he trained himself to give 99½% every play, the last half percent would fall into place. Since destiny shined down on him, he wanted to be ready to produce whatever was needed to play. Every day he would think, "This is my last time around. If I don't do it, I am going to give up. I hope it is in God's will for me to be and I'm blessed with enough talent to achieve."

Each day started at six o'clock in the morning. He would get up, say a prayer, put on his sweats, grab his reminder (football), and head for the streets for at least three miles. He wanted to think of himself as being like the sun, regularly rising each morning. Many mornings the rain would be pouring like the water falling off a high cliff. Some mornings the snow covered the ground like a white blanket. The weather reporter some mornings announced the temperatures to be below the freezing point. That didn't stop the determined athlete as he loosened up. Some neighbors sitting in their parked cars that wouldn't start because of the cold weather shook their heads as Sowell jogged by. Some neighbors thought that he was like clockwork: "Six thirty, here comes Sowell again." Some smiled and waved. Others thought to themselves, "The Sowell's have a crazy son."

Knowing people were making fun of him made Sowell work even harder because now he would have the opportunity to have the last laugh. He often wondered if they would laugh and say he was crazy when they watched him on national TV, playing professional football. Everyday he tried to push himself the last mile of the run. After the three-mile run, he walked for a couple of blocks to warm down. He was then into the kitchen for a full course breakfast that consisted of four to five eggs, two types of meat, hot cakes, five pieces of bread, grits, a glass of juice, and a tall jar of cold water. Sowell would then go back to bed before many had even though of waking up.

The afternoon hour was weightlifting time. He would set his bench out in the yard and work out until the pain was so strong that he couldn't manage to lift his arms or legs, bench pressing over 250 pounds, curling over 150 pounds, squatting over 300 pounds, broken down into many sets with little rest between each one. Sowell called friends to work out with him at Arlington Park School, minutes away from his home. They all had dreams of someday being thought of as a celebrity. They all played as if they were professional players and had thousands of fans watching them. Sowell felt he must work himself until it hurt. Having quit the job his aunt had helped him obtain, unloading trucks at a clothing warehouse, his tryout had to be for real. He knew only all-out effort could get him to where he wanted to be.

Many nights Sowell would be unable to sleep, so he would awaken with a wet face from the tears of failure. Things seemed to be going for the worst. He'd get out his bible and read a few verses, and then he'd get up, put on his weight jacket, and grab his football that always rested beside him. Sometimes it would be two or three o'clock in the morning, but he would start jogging and silently praying that it was God's will for him to succeed. Late at night, sometimes after jogging miles, he'd slow down and walk a little. Many of his so-called friends coming from parties would spot him and throw cans, bottles, and other things out of the car windows at him. When he'd see them again, he wouldn't say a word; he just kept on going. In the back of his mind it made him want to try even harder because some day he wanted them all to regret the way they had treated him.

As the word got around that Sowell had a tryout with the Miami Dolphins, many people didn't believe it. Most said he was just living in a fantasy world and he was not good enough to play pro football. He ignored all of the negative comments. Sowell wasn't going to let fear keep him from his dreams. In his mind he had to take advantage of the chance God had given him, no matter what anyone said. He felt his chances were good.

Sowell decided his goal would be whatever it took to make the team. Never again did he want to resort to throwing papers or be on the welfare role, as he once was. He wanted to be able to help others, instead of having to go to them to get help. He did not want to be ashamed of where he came from and too proud of where he was going. As time drew near to take off for Miami, Sowell wanted to feel like he was in the best possible shape for his tryout. In the last two weeks, he turned into a real psycho—morning, noon, and night was football. He ate, drank, and thought football constantly.

Sowell knew working out was the only way he was going to make it. Psycho conditioning consisted of up at seven in the morning to three in the evening. He'd jog a mile, and then he'd run ten forties and do some backpedal drills. He would go to his old elementary school, South Mifflin, or jog two miles to the high school, Mifflin, and work out on the field. He would then jog home, eat, and start on weightlifting: bench presses, military presses, squats, curls, push-ups, sit-ups, and burn-out drills that consisted of any movement of the body until the pain began to burn. He rested until able to jump rope and run in his weight jacket. He did all of this to keep his body strong. The only fear he had was being burned out when he got to camp, but that was a chance he had to take.

"Near the end of my training, I had to let some of my friends go because they felt I was living a fantasy. I didn't get angry when they didn't come out with me. I felt this was something I had to do alone, if that's what it took. In the previous workouts, they helped a great deal. I would check them while they pretended to be an NFL receiver. For them the games were over and they had to get out and look for a job to support themselves, so I understood that they couldn't come out and play 'chase the dream' with me every day," Sowell said.

HORACE JORDAN SR.

"When I left for camp, I was 5'10" and weighed 167 pounds but was strong for my size. I didn't feel my legs were too weak now." Sowell, in spiritual, physical, and mental condition, was finally prepared to depart for the Miami Dolphins preseason camp—and hopefully not let his psycho conditioning be in vain.

CHAPTER 7

A VACATION

Sending an unemployed dropout on his dream vacation proved to be more costly than planned for the Miami Dolphins and opposing teams in the NFL. Sowell turned his two-week planned vacation into a permanent home.

"I was just sending him on a two-week vacation because they needed another player in camp. He would always tell me he could do it, and he did. I didn't really think he would make the team. I felt he was an average ballplayer that had determination. I was one of the most shocked people when I heard they were going to keep him," said former Buffalo Bill speedster Elbert "Golden Wheels" Dubenion and then Miami Dolphin scout, when asked about his feelings of Sowell before he sent him to the Dolphins camp.

Upon arrival to the camp, Sowell kept thinking of riding the plane back home, only this time as a Dolphins player. He imaged himself as someone important flying down to a big meeting. At that time he was just another passenger on the plane. Nobody tried to talk to him or get his autograph, but he felt this would be his last trip anywhere as a normal person. Nobody on the plane knew who he was, where he was going, or why he was going somewhere. It didn't seem to make any difference to anyone.

When Sowell arrived at the Dolphins camp and saw some of the players who he would have to compete with for a job, he began to realize how hard of a task it was going to be. Seeing players that he had watched running over people and tackling the best running backs, he could only wonder what was in store for him. His mind was focused on the defensive backs he had watched on national television and those he said he could play just as good as, if not better.

Many of the free agents, just like him, seemed to shy away from the other players. Not too many players were eager to hold a conversation with the free agents because they weren't expected to be around too long. The veterans and draft choice players seemed to mingle and talk of their college days, while the free agents sat and waited their turns to show they were there for a purpose. Sowell, who had experienced that feeling before, decided immediately that he wasn't going to let the team and players turn him away from his dream, as once happened in childhood.

After being shown to his room and given instructions, Sowell felt a little more at ease. He noticed the sixth-round draft choice wide receiver from the University of Louisville, Mark Clayton. Sowell wanted to be friendly but didn't dare get too attached to the rookie receiver because he knew Clayton could be one to help make or break him in practice. Neither said much to the other that first day, for they both could feel that anticipation of putting the pads on and showing their football talents on the field.

That night Sowell couldn't sleep well, imagining Coach Shula praising him for a fine job he had done. Sowell took out his bible and read for a while. He then prayed himself to sleep.

When Sowell woke the first morning of practice, he got up and went over in his mind the different skills he had learned over the years. He knew that from this day on that if he didn't do better than the others, he wouldn't catch the coaches' attention, and that would mean an early flight back home. He knew that every day with every play he would have to do something to show he was capable of being on the team. His work was already cut out.

While sitting in the locker room, adjusting his equipment, Sowell listened to some of the veterans boasting about how they knew they already had their jobs won. Of all the bragging that was going around, one person stood out in his mind. He listened to one of the top receivers, Duriel Harris, as he boasted and bragged about how he was going to get all the free agent defensive backs cut. In Sowell's mind grew the burning desire to make Harris eat his words. Sowell was determined not to let him be the factor in deciding if he would play or get cut. His heart was set on getting Harris.

One day in practice, while Sowell was covering Harris, Dan Marino threw the bomb and Harris beat Sowell and made the catch for a touchdown. That not being enough, Harris wanted the rookie to look bad and remember he got burnt, so he spiked the ball in Sowell's face. This hurt the free agent's pride and made him realize that he was in the big times. Sowell then lay back like a tiger, waiting for his prey, and when the first opportunity arose, Sowell came up and caught Harris with a perfect forearm that sent Harris to a quick seat on the grass. Looking down at Harris, Sowell felt confident and knew he had given Harris and the coaching staff something to think about.

Reporters started watching and taking notes on Sowell because he seemed to always be in the thick of things. He set blistering paces in the team's annual wind sprint competition and won the defensive back races, which ended when he collapsed from overexertion.

Pushing himself to the limit was what Sowell had planned, and pushing himself to the limit was what he did. Little did anyone know, but Sowell was on his way to earning a job that thousands had applied for but only a few had been hired to do. During a practice session Sowell went up to Coach Shula and asked for his autograph. Coach Shula, being pleased with the athlete's performances to that point, told him to stick around and he'd give it to him later. And that's what Sowell planned to do: stick around.

As time went on, Sowell began to get noticed more and accepted by teammates. Rookies Mark Clayton, Mark Brown, and Sowell began to become close friends. They all accepted that they had to do what was needed to get the job. The first cut had passed, and they were still there. Though training camp was one of the most strenuous and demanding programs he had experienced, Sowell was glad to be there. Although one of the smaller ones on the team, Sowell was packed like a bomb, and every chance he got to explode, he did. Time and time again he would turn heads as he made a bruising tackle or interception in practice. Many times Sowell would get burnt or miss an assignment, but he would get right back in the thick of things and give it his all, always hustling and going to the ball. Even when called by Coach, he would run.

When down to the last cut, many wondered how the little defensive back had made it further than other free agents and college athletes who had tried out during the preseason. "When you see this little guy in practice, fighting, battling, scratching, willing to hit anybody, you can see why he's caught everybody's attention," Coach Shula said.

On the day of the last cut, when the roster had to come to the best forty-nine players in camp, Sowell kept moving around in the locker room, unable to keep still. He knew this was the big day. Just hours away he would either be Robert Sowell Jr., a player who had a tryout in Miami, or Robert Sowell Jr., player on the Miami Dolphins.

Sowell's mind drifted back to many situations that had led up to this moment. He remembered waking up early in the morning, in fear of being called to the office to turn in his play book; practicing in the hot sun for hours each day; watching great players come and go; and being laughed at when he first showed up and could say he played only one season of football at Howard University. All the odds seemed to be against him, but he was still there. The thought of knocking himself out when tackling a ball carrier and throwing himself into the wedges made up of three or more players outweighing him by one hundred pounds gave him the vision of having done all he could do. But would it all have been worth it if Coach Shula were to call him out and tell him he had done a great job but the Dolphins couldn't use him? This could happen even after the Redskins game, where he had led the team in tackles and Coach Shula called it "the best game I've seen a player have on special teams."

The fear of being cut was turning Sowell's stomach upside down. Every player left looked around and hoped they weren't one of the ten who would have to seek employment elsewhere. It had boiled down to every man for himself.

When Sowell was called into the meeting room with forty-eight other players, he knew that God had blessed him to make the team. The meeting was opened with, "You are the final forty-nine players that will make up the Dolphins team." Players began to scream and holler with happiness. They greeted each other with joyous hugs and handshakes. The feeling of now being a unit was in the air. Each began thinking of the other as a new family member. For Sowell, the small free agent, it was a dream come true.

For a while Sowell just stood there in a daze, not realizing he had finally gotten what he had worked so hard for. All he had done had finally paid off. His new teammates came to greet him and help him enjoy his achievement. Players were saying, "You made it, so you are part of the team now." It was like talking to a wall because Sowell was still in shock. He was floating on cloud nine. If people could have felt what was going on inside of this athlete's body, they might have been electrified. Sowell, not knowing what to do, hurried and called his parents to tell them the good news. He called a few close friends as well, to share the joyful occasion. This was a major step for him, but to keep what he had, he knew he had to continue to produce.

Sowell and his teammates now were able to venture from behind the training camp gates. That meant first finding a place to live. After camp was over, all players were required to find living quarters. Rooms were not provided after preseason camp. Sowell, with help from his new agent, found apartments close to the practice field. Other Dolphins players also stayed in the complex during the season. For the first time in his life, he was on his own and taking care of himself without financial problems. His contract was for the league minimum, but for a man doing what he liked and getting paid for his performance, it was like having a million dollars.

It took about two weeks for Sowell to come down to earth and realize what was really going on. Training camp was over, but he was still at the start of a long journey to making a good impression in the NFL. Now he had to prove he was worthy of the position. Many others had come and gone, some not having the slightest idea why they couldn't beat a free agent rookie out of a job that meant a big paycheck.

With training camp over, Sowell looked back on the past and realized he did deserve to be placed on the official roster. Sowell being one of the smallest players on the team, was called a Smurf. But Sowell played like a big man, taking on anybody and everybody in practice and running at high speed until many times collapsing from exhaustion. He was always trying to be, if not the best, close to the best at everything he did. Sowell showed no fear and no personal feeling for his body when in preseason games, where he would run at top speed and throw himself into anybody. He knew he had made the team for his special teams play. It was not often that a player could exercise his talents enough to be chosen for the team from just limited time on special teams.

To the fans in the stands and viewers at home, special teams plays were the most exciting plays of the game. To the players on the field, these were the most dangerous plays. Most players and coaches felt it took a player with "loose screws" to excel as a defensive player on special teams. It consisted of a situation with every man running toward each other at high speed, usually with thirty to forty yards of built-up speed, and then crashing into each other. Special teams had been labeled as suicide missions because so many injuries occurred during those plays.

To hold down injuries, the elimination of special teams plays were considered, but Sowell was glad it was still a part of the game. "I don't think I'm crazy or have a problem because I primarily earn my pay for my special teams play. I know that's how I got in the door, and if I want to earn a job in the starting lineup, I have to keep producing here or I'll be right back out of the door before I really get a chance. When I go down on special teams, kick off, or punt, I am thinking of making the tackle and hopefully causing a fumble or a turnover. I know a serious injury could occur on any play when I run down, but I feel if I'm going to get hurt, I want to get hurt while doing my job. If you are just jogging and you get hurt, you might feel that if you had been doing your job, the injury might not have occurred. If the coach watches the film and sees me get hurt doing my job the way I'm supposed to do it, he will sympathize with me. But if I'm loafing, he will chew me out and make it seem like it was my fault. I've always watched the special teams play, but I never knew what they went through to make the play. Yes, it's dangerous but its football," Sowell said about special teams plays.

As Sowell prepared for the opener of the regular season, he concentrated on doing his job. No more confinement of training camp—it was time to be a man and show what he was worth. The once-unemployed rookie player who came to Florida for a vacation was now a Miami Dolphins football player living a dream come true. He now had an opportunity to show all the people back in Columbus, Ohio, and other cities that dreams were made from hard work and faith.

CHAPTER 8

LONG SHOT INTO PLAYOFFS

"He's a long shot. We'll give him a traditional quarterback number because he won't be around too long." This was truthful thinking for the Dolphins' coaching staff upon Sowell's arrival. But now the Dolphins organization realized the free agent rookie was for real.

By exerting himself in preseason camp and showing reckless abandon on special teams in preseason games against the Dallas Cowboys, New Orleans Saints, Washington Redskins, and New York Giants, the staff decided with time and continuous hard work that Sowell could make not only a good special teams man but a good defensive back as well. Showing consistency in the preseason games and improvement in practice sessions, Sowell was now ready to open the regular season as a Dolphin on owner Joe Robbie's employment roll.

The sixteen-game regular season schedule opened for the Dolphins in Buffalo on September 4, 1983. Playing the Bills as a Dolphin was the beginning of a journey for Sowell. With the change of uniform number from nineteen to forty-five, Sowell felt he had started to prove what so many felt he couldn't. Now he was here, so he wanted to make believers out of all who doubted him. With what it took to get there, he intended to stay.

While preparing for the flight to Buffalo from his two-bedroom apartment, Sowell felt a feeling of adulthood. He finally was doing for himself. As he left his apartment building with some of the other players, he felt good when he heard some of their fans howling, "Good luck guys. Hope you win." Sowell felt as if he could win the game by himself. He was just that fired up. The flight was the most comfortable flight since his departure from Columbus, Ohio, to Howard University in 1979. He could remember the flight to Miami, with the butterflies from anticipation of making the team. He had called it, and now it was true. He wasn't just Robert Sowell; he was Robert Sowell, a Miami Dolphins football player.

When the team arrived in Buffalo, New York, fans greeted them at the airport, asking for autographs and pictures. Veteran players were the most sought after. Many didn't know Sowell yet. When they arrived at the hotel, it was the same thing: fans, fans, and more fans. For the rookie it was unbelievable. He had never dreamed of the fame the professional athlete really received. He could only imagine that somebody would be after him for autographs and pictures. Playing only limited time on the special teams and getting a little work as the nickel back on defense, Sowell was still glad to be a part of the team, even if he wasn't widely known yet.

When Sowell went out to warm up, he could feel the tension building up because this was for real. Now each game would count toward a playoff or even a Super Bowl berth.

After a short pep talk, the whole team charged out onto the field. When the crowd of 78,715 in Rich Stadium, which was capable of holding eighty thousand fans, began to roar, Sowell felt every cheer was for him. He was so fired up that he tackled one of his own linemen! Though he had played four preseason games—first in Dallas, where he had three tackles on special teams, a second game in Miami against the Saints, a third at Washington, and a fourth against the Giants—those games didn't have the impact of this first regular season game.

At the 1:00 p.m. kickoff time, the teams set up to open the season. The Bills were rebuilding. The Dolphins were coming off a 27–17 loss to the Washington Redskins in Super Bowl XVII. The Dolphins took an early lead and played good, hard defense as they recorded a 12–0 shutout. Watching mostly from the sidelines and waiting his turn to go in on special teams, Sowell was just pleased to be a part of the team.

The next week the Dolphins were in the Orange Bowl, hosting the New England Patriots. Many of the fans in Miami would be able to watch him play. He knew he would begin to get noticed then. Before leaving for the game, some of his neighbors told him good luck. They would be there to watch him play. Sowell had a good week of practice and felt that would help him have a sound game. To open the game, he dashed down the field like a bolt of lightning and made the tackle on the Patriots' kick returner. The roars of 59,343 fans in attendance electrified Sowell until he had to be reminded that he had to come off the field until it was his time again. This game wasn't like the first; it was a showing of offensive explosions. From the sidelines Sowell put himself in each situation and tried to figure out what he would have done if he had been in the game at that time. With a 2–0 record, he couldn't believe the way people were already discussing a return trip to the Super Bowl, which would be all right with him.

In week three the Dolphins prepared to travel to Los Angeles to take on the Raiders. Sowell's plans were to watch and learn the tricks and trades of the Raider secondary, one of the most feared in the NFL. Being able to see some of his old teammates and friends he had made the previous year at Sacramento was a thrill. Knowing he had made it and many others hadn't made him count his blessings.

Just as the 57,796 fans focused on the game, so did Sowell. When not in the game, he studied the defensive backs, and their bump and run move. Sowell knew this was one of the most effective ways to cover a receiver and get respect, but only if used with perfection. Using it the wrong way could cost the team a penalty or a touchdown, if the receiver got behind the defender easily. Even though the Raiders downed the Dolphins 27–14, it was a learning experience for Sowell. He took the bump and run back with him and used it every chance he got in drills.

Week four brought the Chiefs from Kansas City to the Orange Bowl. Sowell started to really feel like a pro and more confident. He bought extra tickets and handed them out to some of the fans who weren't able to afford to get tickets but still rooted for the team. The whole stadium watched the Dolphins get back on the winning track. With fans screaming and howling, Sowell went down and made a perfect tackle on the kickoff. He began a habit of making tackles for special teams. The game ended a low scoring game, but it was enough to give the Dolphins their third win in four outings, as they squeaked by the Chiefs, 14–6.

The previous week Sowell had gone out looking for a car. When he found one he liked, he told the salesman and informed him he was employed by the Dolphins as a football player. The salesman didn't believe a fellow looking like he didn't weigh over 175 pounds could play pro football. He told Sowell he couldn't get the car because he didn't have a credit rating in Florida. Sowell went to another lot and found a car he liked even more, a 1978 two-toned silver and black Cadillac Seville. When he approached the dealer, the dealer said, "I've seen you before. Don't you play for the Dolphins?" Sowell smiled and nodded. The salesman told him if he was interested in any car on the lot, he would fix him up. Sowell went and talked to his bank manager, and the deal was on its way. After having seen Sowell playing against the Chiefs, the first dealer called back and told Sowell he was sorry he hadn't believed him and they would work a deal out. Sowell assured him he would be back, but when Sowell returned, he was driving the Seville he had purchased. He told the salesman not to judge a book by its cover.

When Sowell drove to practice in his Seville, many of his teammates teased him. They said a little man always wants a big car. He was teased that all rookies go out and get the biggest and most expensive car they can find. Sowell told them he bought it because it was what he wanted. In the back of his mind, he had dreams of owning a two-seater convertible Mercedes.

In week five the team traveled to the Superdome in Louisiana to take on the Saints of New Orleans. By game time the dome held 66,489 fans. Meeting the Saints again, only this time as a full-fledged Dolphin, made the trip to the Superdome an exciting one. Playing in the Superdome was like a dream for the rookie. Just being there fired him up. He ran with high speed, crashing the wedge and taking on all Saints that got in his way. The Dolphins fell short as they lost their second game of the season, 17–7. The trip home seemed to last forever. When Sowell got home, he felt pain in his body from the fierce play. He soaked his body and rested it for a week of practice, preparing for week six.

In week six it was a rematch with the Bills, coming from Buffalo. A total of 59,948 fans packed in the Orange Bowl for the rematch. Sowell went out early to loosen up for the game. From the first series, it was evident it would be a close but high-scoring game, just the opposite of the first meeting. When the regulation time ended, the teams were tied at 35 each, which brought on the overtime. After a hard struggle, the Bills ended the game with a field goal that sent the Dolphins down to a defeat of 38–35 in the Orange Bowl. It was the Dolphins' second loss in two weeks and the third of the season. The Dolphins, with a 3–3 record, had to regroup.

Though Sowell was leading the special teams in tackles, he felt he could help more if he could develop the skills to help out in other situations. He worked harder on his defensive skills to qualify for a shot as the fifth defensive back (nickel back) on long yardage situations.

On week seven the Dolphins traveled to New Jersey to take on the Jets in Giant Stadium, in front of 58,615 fans. After the overtime loss to the Bills, the Dolphins needed a win to boost the morale of the team. The Dolphins jumped out to an early lead and extended it to down the Jets, 32–14, and get back on the winning track. Sowell finished the game with two tackles.

Next the Dolphins traveled to Baltimore to take on the Colts in front of a crowd of 32,343. It was a much smaller stadium than most but earned more playing time for Sowell, who played as hard as possible. He ran into the wedge at full speed, sometimes being knocked down and getting up to make the tackle.

At the midway point of the season, the fans and coaches were noticing the rookie's reckless play, and they loved every minute of it. His teammates began saying he was crazy. They were nicknaming him because he was a free agent supposedly from nowhere. His favorite nickname was Koeter, after the unknown football player in the TV commercials. The Dolphins ended up beating the Colts 21–7. That brought the team record to 5–3.

Returning home for week 9 against the Los Angeles Rams, the team felt the pressure of having to keep winning to at least get to the playoffs. A total of 72,175 fans flowed into the Orange Bowl to see their Dolphins return after two wins on the road. The Dolphins kept the streak alive, with a 30–14 crushing of the Rams. In this game Sowell could feel the team knew he was doing a great job on special teams because he didn't have to go down and tear through players. They were coming straight at him. It didn't bother him a bit. He loved the extra challenge. The Dolphins now had a record of 6–3.

Sowell grew closer to his teammates, and they began to take him to their homes and businesses and introduce him to people in their personal life. Around the complex the fans would hang around and compliment him on his fine play.

Week ten was a flight to San Francisco's Candlestick Park to play the 49ers in front of 57,832 football fans. Sowell's work was cut out for him.

He trained harder because now he knew the teams were trying to wipe him out before he wiped the wedge out. He felt the call and answered with still another tackle on special teams. He felt that even if he didn't make the tackle or burst the wedges, he was still making the play because other teams were adjusting their return to stay away from him. It was a close, hard-hitting game, but the Dolphins prevailed and captured a 20–17 win to take back to Miami. The team, now sporting a 7–3 record, with four straight wins, were focused on playoffs and a return trip to the Super Bowl.

On week eleven the Dolphins geared up for a rematch with the Patriots in Foxboro, Massachusetts, in front of a filled crowd of 60,771 noisemakers. The game seemed to last only a short time for Sowell, as the Dolphins fell to defeat for the fourth time in the season. The flight back to Miami seemed to last forever, and Sowell could feel the disappointment of each player. The trip was much quieter when the team had lost. Being a divisional contest, it didn't ease the sting any.

The Dolphins returned to play in the Orange Bowl against the Baltimore Colts on week twelve, and they recorded a 37–0 shutout in front of a crowd of 54,482. Sowell played one of his best games on special teams, with two tackles, one where he almost knocked himself out. Seeing time as the nickel back, he played the corner back position as if he were a starter. After the game fans hung around and asked for his autograph. When he drove away in his Seville, he could hear the fans holler, "There goes Sowell." It was good to hear people were starting to know who he was.

November 23, week thirteen, brought a home state team into the Orange Bowl for a Monday night meeting. The Dolphins, with a record of 8–4, hosted the Bengals in front of a packed house of 74,506 fans, the second largest crowd he had performed in front of, not including the national television viewers and Howard Cosell and the Monday night crew. It was a thrill to meet the Monday night crew and be playing against the Bengals, who were from Cincinnati Ohio just an hour and a half away from his hometown. He wanted to make a good impression on TV and win as a Thanksgiving gift to himself.

The Dolphins had no problems downing the Bengals, 38–14. Sowell had gained attention from the sports world, as they could see why he was leading the Dolphins and league in special teams tackles. With punter Reggie Roby continuing to have great, high and long punts, Sowell was able to cover and make tackles. Monday night announcer Frank Gifford even nominated him for a special teams Pro Bowl pick, but rookies weren't eligible at the time. Sowell, feeling more secure as a Dolphin now and being able to enjoy some of the fame, found it hard to believe the special treatment a professional player received. Many women, hoping he was single, began to put their bids in, but Sowell kept his mind on football and the games ahead.

In week fourteen, the Dolphins went to Houston to meet the Oilers in the Astrodome in front of 39,434 fans. The Dolphins held the Oilers off to post their tenth win, with only four losses, 24–17. With this win and wins in the last two remaining games, the Dolphins would be assured a spot in the playoffs and be the 1983 AFC Eastern Division Champions. Each week to follow would be a process of returning to the Super Bowl. Sowell was already trying to make an impression for the next year.

In the fifteenth week of play, the Dolphins hosted the Falcons of Atlanta in Miami for a crowd of 56,975. Sowell was so fired up knowing they could play in the playoffs that he spent the whole week concentrating on a strategy to haunt teams and make it almost impossible to get past him on special teams. The game went the distance before the Dolphins rallied to win by a touchdown, 31–24. When the game was over, Sowell felt relieved, for he had fought a hard fight. When he came down on punts or kickoffs, he could see one of the largest Falcons on the field coming at him, but his speed and determination got him by.

Preparations for week sixteen, the final week of the regular season, was a heavy load for the free agent who had made a dream come true. The Jets came into the Orange Bowl looking for an upset and wanting to even the score for their earlier loss to the Dolphins. The Dolphins were up for the game, having won their last four. The Dolphins wanted to win and finish the season with a 12–4 record, while on their way to the playoffs. The 59,975 fans were there chanting hours before game time. The Dolphins responded with an easy 34–14 win over the Jets.

It was now off to the playoffs for the AFC Eastern Division Champions. The Dolphins, with a 12–4 record by winning their last five in row, were hot and ready to face the Seahawks of Seattle on December 31. For the veterans it was business as usual. Most had been there before. For the rookies it was the hype of the season. To the former no name, it was a blessing. Sowell had beaten the odds; not only had he made the team and led the league in special teams tackles, but he was also prepared to play in the playoff game. The thought of winning and playing in a Super Bowl danced in his head.

The stage was set for a showdown in the Orange Bowl, featuring the 12–4 Miami Dolphins and 9–7 Seattle Seahawks. It didn't seem to be the perfect match for the Dolphins, Super Bowl finalists last season. The osprey pictured on the side of the helmet was figured to turn to a dejected look. This was just the first time the Seahawks had made the playoffs in their eight-year history. With the powerful explosions, the Dolphins thought they were capable of showing the Seahawks weren't going to survive.

On the last day of 1983 in a soggy Orange Bowl, before 71,032 fired-up fans, the Dolphins took the field, with thoughts of an easy win and being a game closer to Super Bowl Sunday. In the Dolphins locker room Sowell felt he had a role just as important as any other player on the team. Sowell, knowing he would have to play a good game even though they were favorites, wanted to be a part of the Super Bowl team of 1983.

He went out early to get as loose as possible. He had a feeling he would see a great deal of playing time this Saturday. The fans were alive early, as the crowd had already packed the stadium hours before game time. Thinking of national exposure in a playoff helped fire the young man up. Every scream that echoed seemed to be for him alone. The Dolphins would have the ball first, and that would give Sowell more time to contemplate on his job. But what happened in the opening offensive series assured the Dolphins that it was going to be a long day and the Seahawks had come to play. Two tipped passes and continuous pressure made the Dolphins look like they were the underdogs. Waiting patiently on the sideline for his turn to return the favor, Sowell raged with desire to cook a Seahawk duck for dinner.

The two teams exchanged series until two minutes and twenty-one seconds into the second quarter, when the Dolphins scored. The extra point attempt was missed, and the Dolphins were up, 6–0. Sowell took the field to cover the kick. At high speed he raced down the field, but to his surprise, he was wiped out by a blind spot. As he walked off the field, he knew the Seahawks' special teams had not left him out of their game plan. As the half ended the Dolphins had tallied a 13–7 point spread over the Seahawks. In the locker room the Dolphins didn't boast of confidence, as they had before the game, because they knew they had to face the Seahawks in another half, which hadn't turned to duck soup in the fog as planned.

Sowell sat thinking of the blind spot and the three-on-one match he had faced the first half. He wanted to at least get down and bust the wedge, but the problem was he had to keep a sharp look over his shoulder because he didn't know who or how many were coming after him. He sat there thinking of how he was a professional player and how he had earned the name, getting the job done. There was no reason for him to feel that he wasn't capable of doing his job. So he decided in the second half he would have to prove not only to others but to himself as well that he could do the job. A warm feeling ran through his body as he sat up for the opening of the second half.

Sowell raced down the field like a beast in search of a meal, not caring who was in his way. It was back to the reckless play that had gotten him a job, and he not only busted the wedge but got a piece of the tackle. The Seahawks rallied to take control of the game, with a 17–13 lead. With less than five minutes left, the Seahawks almost turned soft and gave the Dolphins the game. At their own twenty-seven-yard line they turned the ball over with an interception. It only took the Dolphins three plays to score and take command, 20–17, with just under four minutes to play. With the score close but time running out, Sowell smelled victory.

On the next kickoff, Sowell blistered down the field, getting knocked down, but returned to his feet and took on the wedge. That not being enough, as the Seahawk return man seemed to be escaping for a score, Sowell returned to his feet for the second time and showed pure determination and whistling speed, running the ball carrier down from behind. The Seahawks used some heroics of their own, as the quarterback connected with the receiver for two long pass gains. This set up a two-yard run to turn the tables back to the Seahawks, 24–20. Finishing off bad luck, the ensuing kickoff was fumbled, and the Seahawks responded with a thirty-seven-yard field goal. At 27–20, with the Seahawks leading, the Dolphins had one final shot to regain respect and move closer to a second consecutive Super Bowl appearance. But it wasn't to be, as the Dolphins also lost the next kickoff by another fumble and the Seahawks ran the clock out. The Dolphins fell prey to the Seahawks, 27–20.

Though Sowell had played his heart out, the pain of defeat sent quivers through his stomach. As he sat in the locker room of the Orange Bowl for the last time of the season, he was reminded not to feel down. He wasn't supposed to have made it that far anyway. Having survived a season as a professional athlete, he had made a dream a reality and given others the hope that they too could beat the odds with hard work. He could now turn his playbook in and return home for a well-deserved rest.

To his surprise when he left the locker room, there were fans waiting for him and his autograph. Players, coaches, and fans remarked on his fine play. He knew then he had gained respect, and all he had done throughout the season wasn't in vain. The loss was painful but also carried a feeling of relief. As he prepared to journey home, he looked forward to coming back for the team banquet. He had come a long way, and he knew the season had to end. He was just thankful it had ended with him being a part of it.

At the team banquet Sowell, dressed in a white tux, black shirt, and black and white hat, experienced the highlight of his season. He was awarded the team's special teams player of the year for leading the special teams in tackles, with twenty. He also helped the league consider the opportunity of a rookie making the Pro Bowl on special teams. If it had not been against the rules, many feel that he too would have been on his way to Hawaii to play in the Pro Bowl. Sowell, a free agent rookie thought to be just another player with a dream, had successfully finished a season after a playoff game.

CHAPTER 9

SUPER FEELING IN
THE SUPER BOWL

The spring of 1984 introduced a new Dolphins team and a confident Robert Sowell. Coming in training camp with a three-year signed contract and a bald head, Sowell wasn't a long shot anymore. This year the rookies would fight for his job, while he concentrated on getting more playing time or even a starting job at cornerback. The killer instinct on special teams still lay in his head, but to add an "S" to the killer bee defense throbbed even more.

This season he didn't just want to be a part of the team and contribute on certain situations; he wanted to be out on the field as much as possible, producing good plays for the Dolphins. He was pleased with the Dolphins signing him again and wanted to show his appreciation where it counted: on the field.

Sowell sported the bald head as a sign of seriousness and used his bump and run technique as a sign of confidence. Even with the signing of a contract, Sowell knew if he didn't produce, someone could take his job, just as he had taken someone else's the previous year. He would use the preseason to prove he was capable of doing the job at cornerback. With close friends Mark Brown and Mark Clayton filling in the starting roles, Brown at linebacker and Clayton as wide receiver, Sowell felt it would be great for him to earn a starting job also.

On September 2, 1984, the Dolphins opened their season at RFK stadium in front of a hostile 52,683 fans. It was like playing at home for Sowell because this was the field he had won his job on the previous year.

49

That day he anticipated a lot of playing time at the cornerback job. After a fine showing in preseason with interceptions, fumble recoveries, and batted-away passes, Sowell felt he was ready to take on the responsibility of covering receivers. The game proved to be a payback match for Super Bowl XVII, where the Washington Redskins had beaten the Dolphins, 27–17. Trailing at the half, 10–7, the Dolphin defense tightened up and the offense started to roll in the eighty-degree heat. Sowell helped spark the defense by covering kickoffs, punts, and receivers as the fifth defensive back on passing situations. The Dolphins used five touchdown passes to beat the Redskins 35-17

On week two the Dolphins were back home to host the New England Patriots. The Orange Bowl was packed to see revenge. The Patriots were the last team to beat the Dolphins in the previous regular season. All 66,083 fans were on their feet almost the whole game. The Dolphins crushed the Patriots, 28–7. It was the second straight victory for the Dolphins. After allowing the Patriots only one score, Sowell felt good about himself and the defensive team. He tried to contribute every chance he got. After the game he was invited to do a radio talk show at one of the local radio stations. This encouraged him to continue to show no mercy on ball carriers on opposing teams. Making tackles on special teams was his specialty, but covering a receiver like a blanket on defense was his goal.

Slipping past the Bills of Buffalo, 27–17, in a filled stadium of 65,455 onlookers, the Dolphins moved to three wins and zero losses. Beating the Bills, the Dolphins had already avenged two of their four last season defeats. Seeing more playing time at cornerback, Sowell could feel the pressure of the players who played most of the game. At times he felt the bend, but he wouldn't break.

Returning to the Orange Bowl for 55,415 fans, Sowell put on a show as the Dolphins stumped the Indianapolis Colts, 44–7, crashing down the field and crushing into the wedge. When not making a tackle on special teams, Sowell bolted receivers at his cornerback job when they attempted to catch a pass in his area. He had come a long way and had begun to look like a versatile player. He ended the game giving the coaching staff reason to consider him for injured cornerback's position.

The Dolphins polished their record to five wins and zero losses by beating the Cardinals in St. Louis, 36–28. The 46,991 fans got to see an explosive Dolphins team. The offense was steady, rolling up points as the defense held the Cardinals offense off long enough to cash in on the win.

Preparations for week six in Three River Stadium had two factors. It was a return trip home for Dan Marino, and the defense faced former quarterback David Woodley. Woodley suffered a concussion on the Steelers' second possession. The 59,103 fans that left not one empty seat in the stadium witnessed the Steelers take a trouncing, 31–7, the worst defeat handed to the Steelers on their home field since 1970. The defense played a big part of the whipping as they returned a fumble for a touchdown, to preserve a 21–0 halftime shutout. Sowell saw a great amount of action and used it to his advantage by making crushing tackles. The hometown showing for Marino was dominating, as the final score showed.

Hosting the Oilers at home, the Dolphins remained the only undefeated team, as the Steelers upset the previously unbeaten 49ers, 20–17. Running backs gave the offense the punch they'd been looking for to compliment quarterback's connection with the wide receivers. After a scoreless first quarter, the Dolphins took a 7–0 lead at the half. In the second half the Dolphins' offense exploded, and the defense allowed only eighty-three yards rushing in, cruising to a 28–10 victory.

Traveling to New England for week eight, the Dolphins scored on seven of nine possessions to show the crowd of 60,711 why they were undefeated and explosive. They netted 552 yards, the most given up by a Patriot team. The game tied at 10–10, the Dolphins scored to take a 16–10 lead at intermission. Making the big plays on defense, the Dolphins defense again complimented the offense, and the result was a 44–24 win for the Dolphins.

At eight wins and no losses the Dolphins hosted the Buffalo Bills in the Orange Bowl. They arose to the occasion and kept the winning streak alive, with a 38–7 bombing of the Bills. Sowell, playing at the cornerback spot, intercepted his first professional regular season pass and had three unassisted tackles. This boosted his morale and gave him the vision of a full-time job at cornerback. But he knew he had to concentrate on his all-around performance.

Playing the New York Jets at home gave the Dolphins a scare, as they trailed for the first time of the season at the half, 10–7. But halftime break gave the Dolphins time to start clicking again. They rallied in the second half to post their tenth straight victory, 31–17, over the Jets.

On the eleventh day of the eleventh month, the Dolphins recorded their eleventh win in a one-point thriller, 24–23, over the Philadelphia Eagles. A blocked extra point, with one minute and fifty-two seconds remaining in the game, gave the Dolphins the win. The 11–0 record was the second best in NFL history, next to the Dolphins team of 1972 that finished undefeated. Down, 14–0, the Dolphins finally scored to draw close. On the ensuing kickoff, Sowell made one of the best tackles he had ever made by rolling down field and hitting the ball carrier with all of his 175 pounds. The shot was so furious that Sowell had to be carried away after knocking himself out with the devastating blow. Being determined, he returned to the game on defense and delivered a blow that caused the Eagle receiver to cough the ball up on impact.

Many began to wonder why Sowell wasn't installed at the cornerback position, since the cornerback was still injured. "I was disappointed about it. I didn't know why. But I went with the flow. I said that as long as they let me come in on the nickel, I'm doing my job. I couldn't let it get me down," Sowell said about it.

Sowell, knowing his team had clinched a playoff berth, knew he would have another playoff game to make a showing in. At Jack Murphy Stadium on week twelve the Dolphins experienced a 34–28 nightmare loss to the San Diego Chargers. It was a heart breaker, as the Chargers prevailed in overtime to give the Dolphins their first defeat of the season. It snapped the sixteen regular season streak of wins, one short of the Chicago Bears of 1933 to 1934. The Dolphins were up 28–14 in the fourth quarter, before the light of an undefeated season was cut off on them.

On November 26 a hostile 74,884 Dolphins fans filled the Orange Bowl to see the Dolphins bounce back from the previous week's defeat and post another victory. Down at the half, 14–10, the Dolphins began their comeback and didn't stop until they had overpowered the New York Jets, 28–17.

Facing the defending Super Bowl champion, the Los Angeles Raiders, the Dolphins experienced disaster from the start. The Dolphins eventually rallied back and only trailed by 17–16 at the half. Both teams exchanged scores before the Raiders cut loose and handed the Dolphins their second loss of the season, 45–34. With two games remaining in regular season the Dolphins didn't dare look too far ahead into the playoffs. They still wanted to finish the season with a convincing record.

In a filled Hoosier dome of 60,411, the Dolphins ripped the Indianapolis Colts apart, 35–17. Leading 17–7 at the half, the Colts appeared to be on their way to an upset and making their season. But the Dolphins, with a second-half splurge, posted their thirteenth win in fifteen games.

As the season grew to a close, Sowell showed he was gaining experience. A total of 74,139 football fans packed the Orange Bowl to watch the Dolphins host the struggling Dallas Cowboys. The game carried a home field advantage throughout playoff, with a win for the Dolphins and maybe a wildcard berth into the playoff for the Cowboys. For the first time in ten years the Cowboys' only showing in the playoffs would be with a ticket and a seat in the stands. Winning at the half, 7–0, the Dolphins held on to post a 28–21 victory, ending their regular play, 14–2, just nineteen points away from an undefeated season. A long but profitable season had come to an end for Sowell and the Dolphins. It set the stage for a rematch playoff clash between the Dolphins and the Seahawks.

The rematch was nothing of a match for the Dolphins, as they smashed the Seattle Seahawks, 31–10, in the Orange Bowl. The Seahawks, going into the game with the best interception (thirty-eight) and fumble recovery (twenty-five) rate, didn't slow down the orange machine. The killer bee defense, only allowed eight first downs and shut the Seahawks out in the second half. It was revenge and left only one more opponent in their way of a Super Bowl date in Palo Alto, California.

The Dolphins did not fear the Steelers, who visited them in the Orange Bowl for a Super Bowl berth. After all, the steel curtain had melted earlier in the season under explosive Dolphins offense. The Steelers seemed to be hungry for the win on their first possession, driving down to the Dolphins' thirty-yard line. But overanxious for an upset, the Steelers fired into the end zone, where Dolphins defensive back intercepted the pass and ran it out to the Dolphins' thirty-three-yard line. The killer bee defense continued to sting and recovered a fumble. Meanwhile the offense was piling up 569 yards, scoring three times in less than three minutes: to give the Dolphins a 24–14 halftime lead. The Dolphins didn't let up and continued to run the score up to a 45–28 victory. Smelling a Super Bowl berth, Sowell became so fired up that he ended the game with a picture-perfect tackle that left a Steelers receiver laid out on the field as time expired.

The Super Bowl match consisted of the two teams with the two best records in the NFL: San Francisco, with a record of 17–1, and Miami, with a record of 16–2. The story would be told January 20, 1985, in Palo Alto, California. On the front cover of almost every sports magazine and in the headlines of every newspaper's sports section were pictures and words of one of the most evenly high-powered Super Bowl matchups. The fire department would have to start putting the flames out early from the hot explosions that both teams were sure to set off. Old record stats from previous Super Bowls would have to be rewritten after the opening kickoff. No person could ignore the electrifying capability both teams possessed. But on January 20, 1985, in Palo Alto, California, only one team could be named the Super Bowl champions. All the fireworks that had been exposed throughout the season were history. All had been a buildup to this the game that every team, player, coach, and owner dreamt of having a hand in. The Miami Dolphins and San Francisco 49ers were it.

Sowell had reached the hype of all hypes. Just two years prior he was an unemployed young man, with only a dream of being on someone's pro football team, and just a year ago he was a player playing in a playoff game. Now he had achieved a great accomplishment. Now a player whose name could be found in the 1983 National Football League media information book was preparing himself for a date in a Super Bowl game. Sowell's trip wasn't to be a free ride to warm the bench. He was going to do a job. Preparations for this game were nothing like any other. The media were tracking down every player they could to get inside information on the game. The players and the press played hide and seek until game time. Many fans headed for California weeks ahead of time, to assure themselves a personal greeting to the teams and start the Super Bowl parties. Fans packed the airport to cheer their team on as the Dolphins went up and away to try and conquer the 49ers and return the championship to Florida. Allowed to mingle and sightsee, the Dolphins took advantage of their free time. But when in practices, the team dared not look too loose. They knew the stakes were high and the winner would profit heavily for their work. The payoff would make every player's pockets heavy. With so much riding on just one game for each player, they played mainly for one thing: pride.

When the team arrived at the stadium, hours before kickoff, they could feel the tension in the cool evening air. By game time the temperature had drifted to the low sixties, but some of the 84,059 fans were still shirtless. As the two teams took to the field, the fans went into a state of hysteria. All watched a historic coin toss that took place in the White House. The 49ers won the flip done by President Ronald Reagan in Washington, DC.

Sowell knew it was showtime as he took his place on the Dolphins kickoff team. The opening kickoff was almost kicked out of bounds. The defense responded by forcing the 49ers to punt. The Dolphins did just what their fans expected on their first possession, and that was to produce points. A thirty-seven-yard field goal put them in the driver's seat, 3–0. The special teams took to the field again. Sowell put his legs in high gear and bolted down field like a ball shot out of a cannon. At top speed he almost overran the play when getting blocked but shifted all his weight and strength to his fully extended arm while on both knees and caught the ball carrier with enough force to bring him down. While catching the runner, he also caught a knee to the head that sent him into a twilight zone. Laid out on the field in the Super Bowl game was not part of Sowell's plan, but it was for a good cause. It happened in the process of doing his job.

The fans were getting nothing less than their money's worth as the Dolphins went seventy yards in six plays. The Dolphins up in score, 10–7, seemed to be unstoppable. But someone lit the 49ers' fuse, and the Dolphins found themselves trailing, 28–10. With one minute and fifteen seconds left in the half, the Dolphins sparked with a field goal, and then with twelve seconds before intermission, they sparked again with another three points, retreating to their locker room still trailing, 28–16.

With darkness setting in, the temperature dropped to the low fifties, and the Dolphins began to lose their sting. The 49ers ran and passed diligently for ten more second half points and stung the Dolphins offense by not even allowing them a spark. It seemed as if the Dolphins had played their Super Bowl game in the first minutes of the contest.

When time expired, the 49ers were a 38–16 winner. It had been a beautiful season that ended in disaster for Sowell and the Dolphins. Still proud to have returned to the game after his early injury. It had been a great game between two teams that together had only lost three of thirty-six games for the season. The pain of the injury and the hurt of defeat still couldn't override the sensational feeling Sowell had. When he walked off the field, knowing he was there and had played was one of the most fulfilling experiences he had ever felt.

Playing in a Super Bowl for a player that had crawled through the back basement window of the NFL was one of the most fulfilling days of Sowell's life. He had reached a dream that most superstars hadn't. Win or lose, he would receive a Superbowl ring, something many great players had never received in their sensational careers. The journey to the Super Bowl was nothing less than spectacular for Sowell and the record-setting Miami Dolphins.

CHAPTER 10

FOOTBALL CHANGED MY LIFE

What once seemed to be an untouchable dream for a young man that wouldn't take no for an answer turned out to be a reality and changing point in the life of Robert D. Sowell Jr. "Playing professional football has changed my life for the better, and I just thank God it was in his will from the start," said Sowell, when commenting on the biggest thing football had done for him. Sowell loved to reminisce about his life before football and during the off-season.

> I'm paying my own bills now, and I'm able to help my family. It feels good to be able to ask my parents what they want and be able to get it for them. My dad asked for a satellite for his backyard. I went out and bought it. My mom asked for a fur coat. I sent out and got it. When my sisters and brother are short on money, I'm able to send them some to help tie them over. I'm not able to give it to them all the time, but if I know they need it, I try to make a way so they can have it. I enjoy taking old friends out to dinner and picking up the tab. When I go to a restaurant, I leave a tip. I remember when I was younger; I would want to go pick the tip up if it was a big one that somebody left. I look at the menu and get what I want. I used to look at the prices and get what I could afford. I have some tailor-made suits that fit me to a T. I

used to wear the same outfit two or three times a week. Now I feel funny if I wear the same socks two days. It's not that I think I'm rich; it's just good to enjoy what you have because one day it could all be gone. When that one day comes for me, at least I'll be able to say I enjoyed it while it lasted.

I really can't say I don't appreciate the way things happened for me, but I wish it could have come easier. I can remember not having a car, and I really liked a few girls, but they said they only talk to guys with a job and nice car. Back then I didn't believe them, but after I came home in my custom Seville, I couldn't keep the women away. Everywhere I went people were blowing their horns and waving; they couldn't tell if I was waving back unless I had my tinted windows down. When I'd cruise through the park, girls would run to the car, begging for a ride. When they found out I played pro ball, they wanted to get married. It was a trip to be able to get just about any girl I wanted just because of my job. People invite me to affairs now and not just plain old parties. When I go, I leave the best possible impression I can.

When I go shopping at the malls, people stop me to talk about football and get my autograph. I love it when I hear a small kid say, "Mommy, Daddy, look; there goes the pro football player Sowell." It just gives me chills, knowing kids look up to me in a positive way. I can remember when a parent would be disappointed with their child if they thought the kid might turn out like I was on my way to being. The kids are so important to me. I guess it's because I know how a child's mind wonders and if it finds something that looks good on the outside, they go for it. Many times that's why they get in trouble. They really don't know the penalty they must pay for doing wrong, regardless if they know if it's wrong or not. I try to set a good example for them to follow. I made the mistake of following the wrong crowd in my younger days. It seemed to be the only way to be accepted. I see now you have people following and idolizing you when you are in the whole public eye. So I try to conduct myself the best I can around kids. When I see them taking drugs or fighting, I tell them they are giving up their chance to achieve their dreams in life. I know I can't change every kid, but if I can show a few the right ways, I feel I have helped society.

It's hard to tell the adults anything because they feel they've lived their life and they don't need to be raised again. When I talk to teenagers and young adults, they sometimes tell me that I think I'm better than them, that since I've made it, I feel I can look down on them. But I don't; I just remember what my elders have told me. You can learn from everyone. There is always something somebody knows that you don't. If you take the time to listen and not be hard on people, someday somebody, somewhere, will say something that you didn't know but will be glad to learn.

I listen to the coaches, they are not just people who come in and tell you what to do on the field. I have found them to be concerned with me and the other players' lives as human beings also. When I have a problem, I can take it to Coach Shula or staff. They will sit down and talk to me. I have a bonding relationship with the coaching staff. I know sometimes they have to be hard on me, but they do it to get the best out of me. I was close to my high school coach and his wife, Mr. and Mrs. Bob Orth. I thought they only treated me like they did because I was a good ballplayer. But I see now that there are coaches that really care about players as people. They don't just want them to win on the field but in the real world also. When guys come in and out of training camp, and the coaches make split-second decisions on if they want to give that player a chance, it makes you wonder if they have any feelings for the person. But I now realize they have a job to do when they're out on the field too.

I think about training camp. People think it's easy, but they don't know the half of it. Training camp is like a fire, and you are trying to cool off. You have hundreds and hundreds of all kinds of athletes trying to make it, but only forty-five will. That's the hard part. My number on my game jersey is forty-five, and if I'm the forty-fifth man, I still am a part of the team. It's trying to beat the odds. You can be there today and seem to be doing good, but tomorrow you may be on your way back home. When it's over you feel good if you made the team. The challenge of someone coming in, trying to take your job—I work hard to keep mine because I know I have responsibilities. If I lose my job, you can bet it'll be to someone who put out a great deal of extra effort. If I'm blessed to stay healthy, I'm going to put out my all.

I feel I was put on this earth for something, and I was convinced it was football. Hardly anyone agreed with me. People tripped out on me. You know they couldn't understand what was really going on with me, but I really did understand what I felt inside. Everybody thought I was really going insane and I was losing it. They talked about me being put into a straight jacket. But on the real side, I'm the only one who knew—me and the man upstairs knew what I was capable of doing. That's why I try to be successful now because I never want to go back to those days I had to do all those things the hard way. I did it all the hard way, as far as working out to make it. I knew that was the only way I was going to make it, by working out and praying to God, keeping the faith and believing I could make it while struggling. I could have gotten into drugs and stealing. I used to go out with my so-called friends, and they would set me up in fights. I'd get jumped; it was a trip. I knew that wasn't me, so I had to dig deep inside to get the change to come out. I got back into my hobbies: swimming, basketball, lifting weights, running track, and fishing. These things sure kept a lot of unnecessary pain off my back.

People say the games of football for high school, college, and pro are different, but I disagree with them; it's just better athletes playing at a faster pace. I try to be consistent with my play on the field. That makes the big difference, just being consistent.

I enjoy my teammates; we are like a family. If something goes down with a teammate, we all get involved to help out. It's just like other teams. If a fight breaks out, no matter who's at fault, other teammates back them up. I notice the whole league looks out for each other. When we hear of a player getting hurt or killed or being involved with a crime, the whole league feels the pain. It's like before I came back to camp in 1984. Our team experienced a tragedy with the loss of a teammate to a car accident, just the morning before I overturned my Seville, totaling it into a telephone pole. If it wasn't for the good Lord, the Dolphins would have been wearing two numbers on their helmets in remembrance. Each team faces these tragedies during the season and off-season, and no matter what team is involved, each team feels the pain and loss. We try to take each other out when we are on the field, but that's just our job. When we are not playing in the game, we are the best of friends; we all enjoy watching each other do well.

The fans pump us up. We get out there and perform for them because they pay to see excitement. It's a dangerous game, but its survival. It's my way of keeping myself and my family secure, and as long as I can stay healthy and the fans and Joe Robbie (owner) want to see me play, I will.

When I finish, I hope I'll be financially secure with myself. It just feels good to be able to relax sometimes, without worrying about problems all the time. I don't try to live above others; I just feel I've worked hard for what I have, and I deserve to enjoy it. One day it will all be over, and I want to be able to say, "I, Robert D. Sowell Jr.," enjoyed it while it lasted." I try not to give the impression that I have a big head, but money and fame change us all in one way or another."

For Sowell, a longtime dream that many see but few achieve made a lifetime difference. Sowell hopes one day someone will ask, "How did you make it?" Another will reply, "He did it the hard way, but so ... well."

REST IN PEACE
ROBERT DONNELL SOWELL JR.
JUNE 23, 1961 – JUNE 22, 2015

Coach Don Shula signs game day books before leaving the stadium.

Mark Brown, Mark Clayton, and Robert Sowell
relax with fans before boarding the bus.

Robert Sowell catches fish in his backyard.

Sowell and Horace speaking with youth in school library

TEE SHIRT ORDER FORM: BODY BY PSYCHO CONDITIONING

Sold to:

Name

_____

Address

_____

City _____ State _____ Zip _____

Phone _____ Email _____

** Amount Must Be Paid in Full ***

No COD Orders Accepted

Checks and Money Orders (Made Payable to Positive Youth of the Future)

PO Box 24862

Columbus, OH 43224

Please Allow 4-6 Weeks for Delivery

Limit of Three Tee-Shirts per Order

Indicate Sizes and Amount of Shirts Wanted

Adult Sizes $15.00 Each	S, M, L, XL, 2X, 3X, 4X, 5X
Youth Sizes $10.00 Each	YS, YM, YL
Color	Black and White

No. of Shirts and Sizes

_____

Total Amount Enclosed

_____

Please Include $7.00 per Order for Postage and Handling

Example Order

No. of Shirts and Sizes	1 XL, 2 YL
Total Amount Enclosed	$42.00

Contact information

*email: pyof@aol.com

*website: www.pyotf.org

65

ABOUT THE AUTHOR

Horace T. Jordan Sr. has been a close friend to Robert Sowell Jr. since childhood and has watched Sowell rise from many of the trying experiences recounted in this book. Horace attended The Ohio State University before graduating from Franklin University in Columbus, Ohio. He has been writing since high school, at Columbus Mifflin, where Horace was junior journalist of the year; he also attended a journalism workshop at Ohio University. As a senior in high school, Horace was the editor for the school newspaper staff and sports editor for the yearbook. Horace is the founder of Positive Youth of the Future, a nonprofit youth organization that promotes education and positive attitudes. The organization helps prepare youth to be the leaders of tomorrow. Horace enjoys writing and spending time with family friends and youth group. This book is the first of many more enjoyable books to come.

Printed in the United States
By Bookmasters